TERROR IN THE SKIES

TERROR IN THE SKIES

Capt. Thomas M. Ashwood

STEIN AND DAY/*Publishers*/New York

First published in 1987
Copyright © 1987 by Thomas M. Ashwood
All rights reserved, Stein and Day, Incorporated
Designed by Louis A. Ditizio
Printed in the United States of America
STEIN AND DAY/*Publishers*
Scarborough House
Briarcliff Manor, N.Y. 10510

IN THE UNITED STATES
Distributed to the trade by
Henry Holt and Company, Inc.
521 Fifth Avenue
New York, N.Y. 10175

IN CANADA
Distributed by
Fitzhenry & Whiteside Limited
195 Allstate Parkway
Markham, Ontario
Canada L3R 4TA

Library of Congress Cataloging-in-Publication Data

Ashwood, Thomas M.
  Terror in the skies.

  1. Hijacking of aircraft—Prevention. I. Title.
HE9779.A74   1987   363.2'876   86-42779
ISBN 0-8128-3125-X

CONTENTS

1. The Strong Reaction to Terrorism   9
2. Setting the Stage   15
3. Take Me to Cuba   23
4. Target of Choice   37
5. Horror in the Cabin—A Flight Attendant's Story   45
6. An Ounce of Prevention   67
7. Defenses Against Terrorism in the Air   95
8. The Terrorists and You   117
9. Arab James Bonds or Psychopathic Killers?   129
10. Command Under Fire: The Pilot's Role   141
11. The Worst of Circumstances   159
12. Welcome to the End of the Line   171

TERROR IN THE SKIES

1

The Strong Reaction to Terrorism

There is a sudden, loud explosion; visibility in the cabin drops almost to zero as water vapor combines with dust and debris to fill the air. There is a loud rushing noise, and you notice the oxygen mask whipping around at the end of its tube. As your hands frantically grasp at it, you desperately try to remember the flight attendant's instructions as the plane taxied out. With incongruous concern that you may do it wrong and look like a fool, you instinctively pull at the mask, which begins the flow of life-saving oxygen to your lungs as you hold it to your face, breathing great gulps through your mouth.

You realize that with one hand you are trying to pull yourself upright on the seat back in front of you. Your brain is scrambling, trying to catch up and comprehend what is happening—why you have the sensation of tumbling and falling. Visibility is suddenly clear except for large objects such as purses, coats, and small carry-on bags tumbling around in space, bouncing off the *ceiling*. "My God, we must be upside down," is your first cogent thought.

The screams of the passengers can be heard above the great, continuous rushing noise—it's like a train going through a tunnel—and you realize that the loud voice you hear is your own, crying out in terror. Your stomach contracts into a tight knot—you know you are about to die.

IS THERE AN air traveler, no matter how seasoned, who has not thought such thoughts in the past two or three years? Comfortable in the air-conditioned environment of a modern jetliner, high above the earth and its problems, maybe sipping a cocktail or eating a meal, hasn't every passenger paused for a moment, remembering details from a news report of an airliner brought tragically to earth by a saboteur's bomb?

Indeed, how many in these mid-1980s have not covertly scrutinized fellow passengers in the boarding area prior to flight, looking for the sign that would betray the presence of a hijacker, a terrorist among those waiting to get airborne. What about that fellow over there by the boarding gate? He seems nervous and keeps looking at his watch. His features are definitely Arabic in their cast, and he is carrying a good-sized bag with him. Wait a minute, he could be a Jew, of course; many Jews have that café-au-lait Mediterranean tan, and as for his frequent glances at his watch—maybe he is nervous of flying and is subconsciously transmitting it to you.

You think you are being a fool, but on the other hand who can be sure these days—who indeed?

Air travelers in the eighties must all, to varying degrees and

The Strong Reaction to Terrorism

with personal variations, go through such thought processes and maybe even project them into anxieties. Through the mid-1980s, terrorism has been escalating in magnitude and quantity in a seemingly endless curve that always points in one direction—skyward.

To understand what is happening and why, one must go to the modern roots of terrorism, for its practice is as old as so-called civilized man.

In the context in which we speak, the people of the world can be divided into the haves and the have-nots, the possessed and the dispossessed, those who would impose dogma on others and those who would resist such impositions. Each of the less desirable categories on its own is cause for antisocial behavior or even violent action or, perhaps, reaction. Being a have-not, a dispossessed, or one who would impose his dogma on another is sufficient unto itself, but combine any two or, moreover, all three and you have the makings of a terrorist.

As Americans, it is fashionable to think of those in such categories as essentially Middle Eastern in geography, ideology, religion, and ethnic origin. This narrow but understandable view is because of the fact that the vast majority of terrorist acts that are committed against Americans or American interests are Middle Eastern in origin. Many of us, and especially those with the requisite ethnic background, tend to think of the Irish Republican Army with a kind of misty-eyed, romantic sentimentality. Visions of Victor McLaughlin come to mind as the tough but kind patriot, fighting for his country against the bloody British (whom we kind of like, too). Millions of dollars annually are collected in the United States for "the Cause" in that little emerald isle across the sea.

The money provides the wherewithal for sadistic gangsters

to cold-bloodedly and carefully shoot a victim's kneecaps to pieces, men and women, leaving them hopeless cripples. It provides for vicious killers who shoot children in their cots and cribs and blow mothers and grandmothers to pieces with bombs in supermarkets and movie houses.

Like it or not, they are as much terrorists as those who hijack and sabotage U.S. airlines in Europe and the Mediterranean and, indeed, many if not most of them, get their training and some of their support from Syria, Libya, and Iran. A network of terrorist training camps has spread throughout the Middle East in what has to be the most diabolical assault on noncombatants in history.

Whatever the nationality, nine years as a combat pilot and sixteen years of involvement in antiterrorism has taught me that the ones to fear are not those with a short fuse and a temper to match. The slow, careful simmering heat of a patient enemy is far more deadly than a brief show of pyrotechnics.

One may argue that the bombings conducted on massive scales against civilian populations in World War II qualify as terrorism. In my view, they do not, for the Allied and Axis nations were engaged in an all-out war, and *neither* side acknowledged the existence of noncombatants.

Terrorism kills but a relative few; in 1985, 928 men, women, and children died as the result of terrorist attacks. Why then, all the fuss? Why all the reaction? Before that question can be answered, the reaction has to be defined.

AS IN MOST crisis situations that threaten life and limb, reaction to the event or events tend to follow predictable patterns. The immediate post-shock kind of reaction is angry and vola-

The Strong Reaction to Terrorism

tile. There is a tendency on both an individual and national level to figuratively run around huffing and puffing and demanding revenge.

The rhetoric that follows a terrorist attack is important, however, for rhetoric allows us personally and nationally to get it off our chests—to vent some steam; to release some anger. Once that emotional head of steam has been relieved, we can start taking logical steps and making plans to find solutions and, yes, even a means of revenge.

Most of us, through self control, learn to respond somewhere halfway between these extremes. We go through the emotional rage and its display, but quickly our intellect takes over and a planned response begins. The speed of the change from hot to cool usually takes longer when a national response is involved. The hot fires are fanned by the media, which assail us from all sides with gruesome detail and endless coverage. This is an area that deserves a book all of its own and is discussed in some detail later in this one.

Along with the rest of right-thinking people, the airline pilots of the world became angry, too, at the increase in terrorism, especially when civil aviation became the target. Following the anger came resolve, and we settled down and tried to find a solution to the problem.

Yet again one must look at the numbers and gauge the response: in 1985, 690 terrorist attacks worldwide produced 928 killed and about 1,500 injured. That is considerably less than the average murder and injured tally for an average year in a medium-sized metropolitan city.

Again, one must ask why then such a reaction to this terror?

2

Setting the Stage

Anticipation can be agony or it can be bliss. The sweetest memories of childhood are the nights before Christmas, a birthday, graduation.

Agony is waiting for the other shoe to drop. It is witnessing vicariously through the news media the plight and suffering of others *in conditions you may well find yourself in* and waiting for the same fate to befall you.

Of the 928 victims who perished in 1985, 23 of them were Americans; and yet, despite that relatively small number, the American reaction was the greatest in all senses of the word.

Now one may ask why? This seemingly disproportionate reaction to such limited terrorist events was evident in the early months of 1986. On April 2, 1986, an explosion occurred aboard TWA flight 840, a Boeing 727, while enroute from Rome, Italy, to Athens, Greece. The device detonated while the aircraft was descending through fifteen thousand feet on its approach to the Athens airport. It blew a hole approximately four feet in diameter in the right side of the fuselage. One man was killed instantly by the explosion, which was directly beneath his seat, and a grandmother, mother, and baby were sucked out through the hole and fell to their deaths upon impact with the ground.

This attack on a single U.S. airliner flight resulted in the death of four Americans. It literally caused panic in the American traveling public. Within a few days, bookings to central and south Europe and the Mediterranean area dropped by 35 percent, and cancellations of previously booked vacations to the same regions dropped by a like amount. A few days after this obscene act, a bomb went off in a West Berlin discotheque, killing four and wounding many others. Two of the dead were American servicemen. Bookings then dropped off to 60 percent, and cancellations jumped to 50 percent.

In relative terms and in a detached examination, two bomb attacks with a total of eight dead, six of them Americans, does not seem to warrant such a massive response from the American traveling public.

Psychologists and other observers of human behavior have sought to find the reason behind this extraordinarily disproportionate response. Was it fear of dying that kept Americans away? The answer must be: probably not, for in our modern society we have developed a bewildering variety of ways to die suddenly and violently and, moreover, we do it in great numbers.

Setting the Stage

Almost 45,000 were killed on U.S. highways in 1985—do you know anyone who permanently garaged his car as a result? About 11,700 died by slipping in bathtubs or from other falls—I have seen no mass rejection of bathing. And 1,900 of us died by gunshot wounds, but gun laws continue to be defeated in Congress.

According to official predictions, New York City will have enjoyed the benefits of hosting some eighteen million tourists in the summer of 1986. New York's murder rate is 20.2 per hundred thousand population set against London's rate of 2.2 per hundred thousand. All of Greece has a rate of 1.7 per hundred thousand and Spain 1.1 per hundred thousand. In short, one is in more danger from the antics of drivers in France, Greece, Italy, and even London for that matter, than from the operations of terrorists. Although the drivers have no political motive and surely do not intend to kill or maim innocent men, women, and children, they are regrettably considerably more successful.

Let us examine the incident most authoritative people credit with the vacation panic of 1986.

When details of the explosion on board TWA flight 840 were widely published by the news media, who among us did not stop and think what it would feel like to be sucked through a hole in the fuselage of an aircraft and fall screaming for two miles to die upon impact with the ground. Whose imagination did not at least fleetingly toy with the image of that plunge, the spinning earth rushing up to meet you? It gives you a shiver to think about it, doesn't it? It gets us right deep in the gut and lives there for a long time, not soon to be forgotten.

Therein lies the answer. Terrorism is so deadly effective

because most of us are chilled by the knowledge that a bizarre fate could befall us in the most mundane circumstances, in the most ordinary place.

Have you noticed that the new genre of horror movies, which are intended to scare the bejesus out of you (and usually do), have eschewed the old haunted house scenarios of the horror movies familiar from the beginning of cinematography through to the seventies? Instead, the action takes place in ordinary suburban homes and towns. Summer camps have become popular settings, too. The victims are ordinary people, mostly nubile teenagers, but easily identifiable with normal, bucolic American life. This, as those clever directors and producers have discovered, is what makes their product so much more *terrifying*.

There you are, sitting in an aircraft miles above the earth, or you may be enjoying a vacation of sun and sea on a cruise ship, realizing the vacation of your dreams. Or can you see yourself sitting at a sidewalk café, sipping a cognac and a demitasse, watching the passing parade on the Champs Elysées? Then without warning, *BANG!!!*—and all the images of the bleeding and broken bodies you have seen in the print and video media become reality to you.

A carefully planned and executed terrorist attack will produce a certain, predetermined number of bleeding and broken bodies, which in turn produces the maximum amount of terror in those remaining alive. Too many bodies and too many attacks, and we become numb and even inured to them. Six million Jews slaughtered in Europe in World War II is meaningless to most of us. Not because we don't care—it is simply that we cannot image six million of anything.

You are now looking at a single page: what does six million

Setting the Stage

pages look like? How high would the stack be? How heavy its weight? You can't visualize it, can you? I bet, though, you can imagine what twenty pages look like, or even thirty. I bet that you also have an idea of what twenty-five bodies look like broken and bleeding in odd poses like carelessly discarded marionettes.

This is where they get to us—in relatively small, violent, highly visible attacks. This is how the terrorist does his or her dirty work.

One of the most common experiences we share throughout the world is the modern wonder of aviation. From the multimillion-dollar-a-year businessman winging his way across the world at twice the speed of sound in the luxury of the Concorde to the Portuguese fisherman in coach class, flying from the Azores to Boston anticipating six months of tough conditions, fishing in the rich waters off Newfoundland—they are sharing the common experience of traveling by international aviation.

International Civil Aviation is given the distinction of being capitalized, for it is important enough that the world community body, the United Nations, established a special division to concentrate exclusively on its conduct. In Montreal, Canada, there is a magnificent edifice and an assembly attesting to its special importance to the world—the International Civil Aviation Organization (ICAO).

Stop and think for a moment about the wonder of such international air travel. Not the science or magic of actual flight itself, but the fact that aircraft, people, and goods from practically every nation in the world pass in and out of each of our countries in huge numbers with little hindrance or delay. On any given day there are about three million passengers flying to international destinations on roughly twenty-two thousand flights. Such is the desirability, profitability, and multiplicity of such flights that special treaties are negotiated between nations to place limitations and restrictions to preclude too much flow in one direction or the other. These are called civil aviation bilateral agreements and often take months and sometimes years to negotiate and then renegotiate just two or three years later.

Special multinational treaties exist with the imprimatur of ICAO, three of them specifically dealing with acts of interference with civil aviation—a fancy term for hijacking and sabotage. These treaties, known as the Hague, Montreal, and Tokyo conventions because of their various meeting locales when adopted, describe specific crimes against civil aviation, which the signatories and ratifiers agree not to condone or commit. Alas, the road to civil aviation security is, like the road to hell, paved with good intentions.

When President Carter attended an economic summit meeting in Bonn, West Germany, in 1978, he and the heads of state from France, the United Kingdom, the United States, West Germany, Canada, Japan, and Italy found themselves unable to agree on any substantive economic matters, so they saved political face by bringing home a much-touted accord on air piracy (yet another popular term), attesting to the leaders' pristine image of supporting international motherhood and apple pie.

Here are the grand words describing the grand intentions:

> The seven Heads of State and Governments concerned about terrorism and the taking of hostages declare that their

Setting the Stage

Governments will intensify their efforts to combat international terrorism.

To this end, in cases where a country refuses the extradition or prosecution of those who have hijacked an aircraft and/or does not return such aircraft, the Heads of State or Governments will take immediate action to cease all flights to that country.

At the same time their Governments will initiate action to halt all incoming flights from that country or from any country by the airlines of the country concerned.

They urge other Governments to join them in this commitment.

This so-called Bonn Agreement found others anxious to sign on to its provisions, which in essence stated that if a nation sponsored acts of violence against civil aviation from another nation, then that offending nation would suffer an economic boycott from those who signed the accord. Australia and Portugal later jumped on this particular bandwagon, and many other nations have expressed support.

It all sounded like a pretty good idea at the time—and even now—but the practicalities of ties between a few of the signatory nations and terrorist sponsor nations soon lead to massive scurrying for cover behind interpretations and technicalities to avoid the difficulty of actually having to do something that might damage those ties or, just as bad, attract the terrorist's attention to themselves.

Meanwhile, while all this highly political, highly public, and basically useless activity was going on, a major terrorist group—the Palestine Liberation Organization—was going through one of its periodic internal upheavals. George Habash, impatient with Yassir Arafat's "moderate" stance, which was adopted to encourage international recognition of the PLO cause, broke ranks and formed the Popular Front for the Liberation of Palestine (PFLP).

The Palestine Liberation Organization has spawned a number of subgroups, most notably the PFLP and the Black September group responsible for the massacre of the Israeli Olympic athletes in 1972. Countless smaller acts of terrorism and violence continued in and around the Middle East as local groups took advantage of the situation and, following each case or atrocity, claimed membership or affiliation with one of the Palestinian groups.

Attacks on civil aircraft began to increase.

3

Take Me to Cuba

The first known and recorded hijacking took place on a domestic flight in Peru in February 1931. Little is known beyond those few details, for communications and media attention were sparse back in those days. That may well explain the sixteen-year gap in attacks on civil aviation, for the next hijacking to occur was on July 25, 1947, when three men commandeered a domestic Rumanian aircraft, killed a crew member, and forced it to fly to Canakkahe province in Turkey. In the years up to 1956, twenty-two hijackings took place, many of them causing fatalities to crew members and passengers. All of the hijackings involved the Iron Curtain countries or Red China, and of the twenty-two hijackings, eighteen came *from* those countries. The nations involved were Czechoslovakia, Yugoslavia, Rumania, Bulgaria, Hungary, People's

Republic of China, Poland, and North Korea. While other hijackings to and from communist nations would occur through to the 1980s, essentially this period of the '40s and '50s belonged almost exclusively to eastern Europe.

As that eastern European surge began to wan, on the other side of the world the Caribbean was thrust into hijacking prominence. Closing out the 1950s and featuring largely into the early 1960s, hijackers fleeing from Cuba became all the rage. During 1960 and 1961 there were ten hijackings from Cuba to the United States, with a number of passengers and crew members killed or wounded. I can find no record of the arrest or indictment of those who were responsible. They were, it appears, treated as refugees fleeing from communism and in most cases were granted asylum and given generous assistance in their resettlement.

During the early days of civil aviation security, as chairman of the Flight Security Committee of the Air Line Pilots Association of the United States, I discovered that one of the pilot members of my organization was a Cuban who had hijacked an aircraft in his escape to the United States! He is to this day a pilot with a major U.S. airline. While the revelation was embarrassing it did serve, however, to underscore the double standard of behavior imposed on communist states by their noncommunist neighbors. Indeed, this double standard was a very real obstacle to the vigorous attempts that concerned airline pilots were making to force an international solution to what they saw as a growing threat to civil aviation.

Based upon available data, it seems fair to say that in the period from 1949 through 1961 most of the hijackings that took place were conducted by people who were fleeing from communist regimes to the West. This may well explain why few Western nations seemed concerned with what was becoming, inexorably, a dangerous means of political expression and escape. By and large the people of Western nations seemed unconcerned and, in many cases, greeted the hijackers as heroes. However, while not yet too excited about the situation, airline pilots began to feel some nervous stirrings of anger and concern. The realization that hijacking was to become epidemic had not yet dawned, and the fact that epidemics spare no one, good guys or bad guys, had yet to be recognized.

Thus began the era of the "gunpoint Cuban airlift." From the 1960s through the 1970s, "take me to Cuba" almost became a game—a very deadly game, as the sprinkling of dead and wounded attested to.

There have been two "Cuba airlift" eras in U.S. civil aviation history. As mentioned, the 1960s and early 1970s first thrust hijacking into the consciousness and lexicon of American society. There are a number of reasons why Cuba became the destination of choice for hijackers during this period.

It was (and remains) an enemy of the United States. There were no extradition treaties in existence between the two countries, and it had the benefit of being located a mere eighty-five miles from the coast of Florida and was therefore easily reached by virtually any aircraft in use in civil aviation. In addition, although the image of Fidel Castro had tarnished for most Americans, there still existed some vestige of admiration for him insofar as he had overthrown the Batista regime and appeared to be making great efforts to eradicate the appalling poverty under which most Cubans lived. This appealed to many liberal and socialist Americans at that time.

TERROR IN THE SKIES

Of the scores of hijackings that took place during this period, more than half were committed by fleeing felons or fugitives. The list of charges and convictions of the hijackers reads like a compendium of criminal activity: bank robbers, murderers, drug dealers, burglars, rapists, all saw Cuba as a sanctuary from the American criminal justice system. The Cuban authorities, engaged in a major propaganda war with the United States, were delighted with the embarrassment this uncontrolled flow was causing their giant enemy to the north. At the time they seemed willing to accept the dregs of U.S. society, which ultimately led to a strange turnabout a few years later.

By and large, the remainder of the hijackers during this era were mentally ill people who suffered from a bewildering array of mental disorders ranging from psychosis to schizophrenia. A noted psychiatrist, Dr. David Hubbard of Dallas, Texas, began an intensive study of hijackers at this time. As a result of his work in this field, he subsequently founded an institution known as the Aberrant Behavior Center. His findings revealed some interesting facts about the psychological makeup of hijackers, but his theories lost credibility with airline pilots and others in the civil aviation security field when he insisted that all hijackers, regardless of motive or state of mental health, suffered from the same psychological problems of dominant mothers and visions of flying through the sky like birds.

I worked with Dr. Hubbard, however, and found much of his work useful in preparing the groundwork for what would become the Hostage Negotiating Technique and in preparing crews to handle hijacking situations.

A small but nevertheless significant group of "Cuban"

hijackers at this time were politically motivated Castro supporters bent upon embarrassing the United States. They completed the triad of what became known in the trade as the three C's. The Criminals, the Crazies, and the Communists. During this period, if you were flying anywhere in the United States and especially in the Boston-New York-Miami corridor, you had a small chance of being hijacked by one of the three C's.

A typical "take me to Cuba" hijacking began in one of two ways. Either the hijacker or hijackers would rush the aircraft at the gate so as to overcome whatever rudimentary security existed at the time, or they smuggled weapons on board and later took a flight attendant hostage to gain access to the cockpit and the flight deck crew. There were incidents when the hijacker simply handed the flight attendant a note saying that "this is a hijacking, take me to Cuba" and either showed her a weapon or indicated that he had a bomb concealed in a bag or package.

In many cases, the passengers were unaware of what was happening until just before landing in Havana, a situation that certainly lessened the danger to the flight, for one of a hijacked crew member's greatest fears is a heroic passenger who can turn a controlled situation into deadly chaos.

When the hijacker chose to make his intentions clear by standing up and holding a weapon to (usually) a flight attendant's head and declaring "take me to Cuba," control of the flight was maintained either with the hostage or by his presence in the cockpit with his weapon on the flight deck crew.

Because of Cuba's proximity to the United States the ordeal was short in duration. An average time would be about two hours. As more and more incidents occurred, each subsequent batch of hijack victims became more relaxed and even pleasantly excited, in some cases, at the prospect of a free side trip to Havana.

THIS SEMIPOPULAR ATTITUDE paradoxically became one of the major difficulties in the airline pilots' attempt to get some serious defenses against hijackings. After all, it was reasoned, it's just a question of transportation by Smith and Wesson and no one gets hurt.

Well, people began to get hurt, and people began to get killed. Even more dangerous, perhaps, others throughout the world began paying attention to this phenomenon and saw it as a useful weapon in their own struggle for their own causes.

The Cuban authorities' handling of each situation lent greater force to the cavalier attitude surrounding these hijackings. In almost every case the hijacker or hijackers were led off by armed guards in what was obviously some form of custody, the passengers were generally allowed to deplane while the aircraft was being refueled and were allowed and even encouraged to make purchases of rum and cigars at the airport terminal shop. While they were guarded at all times, it was done in a nonmenacing manner. All in all it was quite a jolly occasion.

Most of the hijackers underwent some form of Cuban justice and finished up in a mental institution, jail, or a form of house arrest where they were to spend the rest of their lives. The handful of politically significant hijackers was accorded warm welcome and was absorbed into Cuban society.

During 1978 the Castro government reached a bilateral agreement with the United States on hijackers and allowed a number of U.S. hijackers to be returned to the United States where they were tried and convicted and sentenced to stiff prison terms. With this event the Cuban hijacking syndrome faded away but did not die.

IN EARLY SPRING of 1980 one of the most diabolically clever acts ever perpetrated by one nation against another was thrust upon the United States by Cuba. This act created the second era of take-me-to-Cuba hijackings but this time the dangers were greatly magnified.

I refer to the Mariel boat lift, so named for the Cuban port city of departure, Mariel. Fidel Castro, stung by the increasingly shrill denunciations of the Carter administration, opened his borders for outbound refugees. Thousands upon thousands of Cuban nationals availed themselves of this window of opportunity and flocked to Mariel to fight and bribe their way on board the most motley fleet of ships ever assembled since the British army was evacuated from Dunkirk in World War II. Every entrepreneur with a craft that could hold people and stay on top of the water (and sadly some that couldn't) seemed to suddenly appear for this gigantic boatlift of those who became known as Marielitos. Seeing the mass of Cubans trying to escape their homeland gave Castro some pause for thought and either by design or simple opportunism, he ordered his jails emptied of those convicted of criminal, nonpolitical crimes and had them shipped out of Cuba to the United States. Taking further advantage of the opportunity, he also emptied out those unfortunates dwelling in Cuban mental institutions and shipped them out too.

The immigration authorities in the United States were

literally swamped by the hoard of refugees who came ashore at various ports and beaches in Florida. As a result, thousands of mentally ill and criminally undesirable Cubans spread out and were swallowed up by the already large Cuban population in Miami and its environs.

Considering that many of them had been forcibly shipped from their homeland and detached from family, social, and even criminal ties and connections, it should have been no surprise that some would try to return from whence they came.

Unfortunately, overwhelmed with the problem of settlement of the refugees, the attention of U.S. authorities was focused in directions other than aviation security as a Cuban problem.

Thus was created the environment that spawned the era of the "homesick Cuban."

WHY WAS THIS era more dangerous than the earlier one? Since the end of that earlier era many significant changes had taken place in U.S. civil aviation. With the signing of the 1974 Aircraft and Airport Security Law by President Nixon, all commercial airline flights had to have pre-board passenger screening. Metal detectors or magnetometers appeared at boarding gates or security checkpoints. Thorough searches of hand baggage took place, to be replaced later with low-pulse X-ray scanning of such baggage. As a result, there was considerable danger in trying to smuggle a gun or bomb on board an aircraft.

When the first abortive attempts revealed the efficiency of the U.S. civil aviation pre-board screening techniques, the ever-resourceful criminal minds sought ways to get around them.

Thus was invented the new and frightening phenomenon of

the gasoline bomb or Molotov cocktail as a hijacking weapon. Bottles of whiskey filled with flammable fluid plus a 25-cent butane gas lighter became the ticket home for many homesick Cubans.

Airline pilot security experts in cooperation with U.S. federal authorities scrambled to find a defense against this latest menace. As an experienced airline pilot and security expert, I thought I recognized the danger of this latest method of hijacking, but it was not until I observed tests conducted on actual aircraft cabins that the enormity of the danger came to light (no pun intended). Flammable liquids ignited in an aircraft cabin, especially when pressurized in flight, create the most rapid and appalling devastation imaginable. The fireball created by this method would unquestionably leave few, if any, alive. The speed of its spread throughout the cabin is a mute but dramatic accusation of the shocking failure of aircraft manufacturers and their customers and the Federal Aviation Administration to provide fire-resistant materials in passenger aircraft. Those who did not die within seconds from burns or seared lungs would die a few seconds later from inhaling the highly toxic fumes created by burning the materials from cabin furnishing. Highly acrimonious and bitter battles are currently being waged by flight attendant organizations, notably the Association of Flight Attendants, and the Air Line Pilots Association to force legislative correction of this problem from the incredibly obstinate triumvirate of government, manufacturers, and airlines.

Victory is still not in sight. As in most matters relating to aviation safety, the stop-light syndrome comes into play: that is, before authorities will install a stop light at a dangerous intersection, a requisite number of children have to get killed.

I am not sure of the requisite body count for the installation of fire-resistant cabin materials, but I am sure it must be very high, for many victims have died in accidents that were survivable except for the cloud of poisonous fumes created by burning cabin wall panels, seats, carpets, and all the other decorative accoutrements in *every airliner's cabin.*

AS WORD OF such hijackings were publicized, more and more attempts were made, sometimes several in one week. The focus for these attempts was almost exclusively Miami Airport.

In response, the Civil Aviation Security Authority, the Air Line Pilots Association, and the airlines determined that security checkpoint personnel would have to examine every bottle or container capable of carrying a liquid. Seals on bottles were checked very carefully, and the bottles themselves were checked to see if they had been sliced open at the base and glued back together. (Israeli aviation security forces recently found a small automatic pistol concealed in a bottle of spirits that had been tampered with in this fashion.) Holding up each bottle to a light is a quick and sure method of detecting the presence of foreign objects in bottles and this check is now standard practice on most international flights.

In concert with the bottle check was a suggestion from the Security Committee of the Air Line Pilots Association that proved to be remarkably effective, especially considering the simplicity of the suggestion: notices in both English and Spanish were posted at all Florida and New York airports at each security checkpoint pointing out what the Cuban authorities were doing to hijackers who chose to return to Cuba in such a fashion. This simple step is credited with a major piece of the reason why the "homesick Cuban" phase quickly became passé.

BOTH OF THE Cuban hijack eras produced some wry and even amusing events. I can recall one excited hijacker jumping to his feet waving a pistol and shouting "take me to Cuba" only to have a quick-witted female flight attendant snap at him that the seat belt sign was still on, so he had better sit down and fasten his seat belt. As the astonished hijacker obeyed, she calmly took the pistol from his hand while scolding him that, "These are not allowed to be carried on aircraft!"

On another occasion, the captain of a hijacked flight, taking advantage of it being nighttime, went through an elaborate charade of pretending to navigate to Havana and speaking with Havana Air Traffic Control and then, with the help of a sharp FAA controller, landed at a southern Florida airport. The hijacker deplaned the aircraft convinced he was in Havana—only to walk into the arms of the local law enforcement forces!

This incident gave rise to a serious study to check the feasibility of building the facade of a facsimile of the Havana Airport Terminal building at a military airport in Florida. While it had the elements of a good idea, it was recognized that its ability to fool hijackers would probably be limited to the first one or two before the story got out and the whole world would know about it. Noting the ability and propensity of the free press of the United States to publish all and everything known about hijacking and defenses against it, the idea was reluctantly dropped.

DURING PHASE ONE of the Cuban hijacking, another bizarre form of criminal activity against civil aviation captured the public's attention and imagination; this was the overpublicized and mercifully brief period of "jumper jacks."

On November 24, 1971, a man identified on the passenger list as D. B. Cooper took over a Northwest Boeing 727 en route from Portland, Oregon, to Seattle, Washington. After landing and obtaining a parachute and $200,000 in cash, the hijacker forced the plane aloft, then parachuted from the ramp exit stairs at the rear of the aircraft somewhere into the wilds of Washington state.

The curious American affinity and admiration for the criminally eccentric bubbled to the surface, and D. B. Cooper passed into the annals of criminal American heroes right up there with Jesse James, Al Capone, Billy the Kid, and their ilk. Immortalized in song and movie, D. B. Cooper today still remains a mystery, for he was never found. A few years back, some money believed to be part of the extortion money was found on the bank of a dried-out river in the Washington state wilderness. FBI Special Agent Ralph Himmelstach, previously assigned to this case, is in retirement, still trying to track down the elusive D. B. Cooper by spending much of his time in a frustrating search of the jump area for any sign of Cooper's body or loot. Other than the aforementioned find, there has been no clue as to what really happened to him.

It was all very glamorous and exciting unless one stopped to think of the enormous danger with which he had jeopardized the passengers and crew members. Most authoritative sources indicate that his most likely fate was death upon landing from his night jump or shortly thereafter, with his remains being disposed of by Mother Nature's clean-up squad of coyotes and other predators—to me, a seemly ending to this affair.

The assumed success and glamorous media attention given to D. B. Cooper triggered an astonishing number of copycat jumper-jack hijackings. Almost exclusively, the victim aircraft was a Boeing 727, which had a rearward trailing, hinged staircase that one could open in flight, walk down, and literally step into space behind the aircraft. To jump from any other type of passenger jet was virtually impossible.

Under pressure from the Air Line Pilots Association, in December 1972, the Federal Aviation Administration issued an order to install speed switches on all B-727s. This device deactivated the opening mechanism in these rear steps when the aircraft was in flight.

This was one of those rare occasions when a simple, inexpensive, absolute solution was found to a specific threat against civil aviation. How many times since have we wished for such success in the war against the myriad of other threats that continue to plague airlines?

4

Target of Choice

To understand why civil aviation has become the target of choice above all others for terrorist attention, one has to examine the abundance of advantages an aircraft offers as a target.

In a world that frequently understands the price of everything and seldom the value of anything, cost is a high factor. Today's price for a new Boeing 747 is around 100 million dollars. A used 747 in good condition would cost perhaps 50-60 million dollars. A new DC-10 is 70 million dollars; a Boeing 727 short-range aircraft about 27 million dollars. One can readily see then that, on the basis of cost alone, a civil jetliner commands attention.

"Ah yes," one may ask, "what do you do with a Boeing 747 once you have stolen it?" After all you can't sell it to a fence. Under such circumstances, an aircraft has no resale value—the threat to destroy it is sufficient for the terrorists' needs.

TERROR IN THE SKIES

I know of no other item costing as much as a plane that can be totally and irrevocably destroyed with a couple of hundred dollars worth of explosives. Designed to withstand the normal forces and rigors of its flight environment, an aircraft is tremendously strong. It can be tossed in violent storms, banged onto runways in rough landings, and stressed in a variety of ways over decades of use and still maintain structural integrity well within the envelope of safety. But place a few pounds of explosives in strategic positions throughout the aircraft's monocoque-construction fuselage, and that big, powerful machine with its thousands of miles of wiring, hundreds of miles of tubing, thousands of rivets, brackets, and aluminum panels can be reduced to worthless junk in seconds; and that's just on the ground.

Bomb damage in flight is far more devastating because of the likelihood of damage to the controls resulting in a crash. In addition, when in flight, the cabin is pressurized to compensate for the higher altitudes it operates at. This pressure differential adds a huge force to that of an explosion, much like the violence of the force when one pricks a highly inflated balloon as opposed to a half-inflated one.

The most graphic example of the destruction of aircraft just for the shock value and without loss of life occurred in Jordan in 1970. Palestinian terrorists had hijacked a Trans World Airlines Boeing 707 from Frankfurt, West Germany, a British Airways VC 10, and a Swissair DC-8 to an abandoned military airport in the desert. After six days the terrorists blew up all three aircraft in an orgy of wanton destruction the likes of which has never been seen before. In today's dollars it would amount to around $120 million. A Pan Am B-747 was hijacked

Target of Choice

out of Amsterdam, the Netherlands, on the same day. Seconds after the landing at Cairo and the emergency evacuation of passengers onto the runway, the aircraft was blown up and totally destroyed. Add another $70 million to the score.

The crews and passengers of the TWA, British Airways, and Swissair flights were eventually all released, but one cannot say they were "unharmed"; for many of them the trauma lasts to this day.

THIS LEADS TO the next feature of civil aircraft that makes them desirable targets: the people on board. There are few better places to find a number of people of a targeted nationality than on a country's national airline, although on any given flight of any international airline the presence of Americans is almost certain. There are so many of them, and few nationals travel more than Americans. There is the added bonus on international flights of the certainty of hostages from a variety of nations, which, indeed, strengthens the terrorists' hand. Hijack an international flight of any major flag carrier airline, and you end up with a veritable United Nations of hostages—each one of them a potential chip in a high-stakes poker game. Adding to the size of the pot is the inevitable presence of elderly, sick, female, and child passengers: all high-denomination markers in this deadly game.

If one accepts that terrorism is the most economical, cost-effective means of warfare, as indeed it is, then what could be more cost effective than taking an enemy in the battlefield of your own choosing. Every military commander's dream is to fight his battles on the turf of his own choosing and with odds that favor him to the greatest degree. To fight one's enemies on their own ground is to place yourself at great risk, for you stand in the midst of the enemy, surrounded and subject to the entire array of defenses of its home forces: military, law enforcement, and civilians. Airlines are recognized as belonging to and representing their countries of registry. Therefore, Pan Am means the United States, Air France is France, British Airways translates to Great Britain.

If one wants to attack the United States, France, or Great Britain, as these examples suggest, then one may do it in one's home territory or any other place in the world where they may fly and where they may be vulnerable. One might say this is cowardly, but it is cost effective. How else can a minor force wage war against an economic and military superior power? Terrorist attacks and the threat of further attacks are costing a fortune in money, causing massive inconvenience in their deterrence, and are beginning to hamper the normal orderly flow of life and commerce. In 1985 in the United States alone, government and private industry spent $42 billion on antiterrorist protection, a growth of 12 percent over the previous year and projected to double in growth in 1986.

It was Shakespeare who said, "All the world's a stage and all the men and women merely players. . . ." Well, the immortal bard would doubtless be astonished today if he were able to see his words come to life in the form of a modern-day airline hijacking. In 1985, when Shiite Muslim extremists took TWA flight 847 by force and for seventeen days forced it to fly back and forth between Beirut and Algeria, it was pure theater to the ultimate degree.

The hijackers who commandeered the Trans World Boeing 727 were the central actors in the play. The aircraft, its crew, and its passengers merely props on the world stage. Those billions of people in the world with access to news media were the audience.

This was the world, this was the stage upon which the hijackers of TWA 847 opened their three-act tragedy/drama. Act I opened with the hijackers seizing control of the aircraft when it was leaving Athens, Greece. The audience was alerted. Moving around the stage, the action moved to Beirut, a city synonomous with wanton death, destruction, and nihilism. The tension mounts as Act II plays itself against a backdrop of changing scenery, Beirut to Algeria and back again, the terrorists, platooning with fresh reserves while the exhausted crew remains center stage. Act II is spiced up by the shooting death of one of the players; flagging audience interest is renewed. Act III ends, after a run of seventeen days, with a whimper as the villains escape justice and melt into the audience.

The very breath of life to a terrorist with a cause is publicity. The sole purpose of the act is public attention. The greater the public, the greater the attention. The Western world is trapped in the paradox of the freedoms of its news media feeding the animals gnawing at the entrails of its pride and resolve. Theoretically, that hijacking (and others like it) could have gone on indefinitely until the media became jaded or other terrorist acts of greater magnitude snatched the spotlight from that obscene act to one of fresher interest or greater obscenity.

Will we have disparate terrorist groups vying with each other? Outkilling and outmaiming in an attempt to obtain more minutes of prime-time television? I fear for the future in this regard, for the behavior of the press, video, audio, and print during TWA 847's ghastly odyssey was, in itself, obscene.

One could keep a Boeing 747 traveling from capital city to

capital city encircling the world like an airborne circus but with the passengers and crew being obliged to perform the death-defying acts of survival. Perhaps an updated version of the tragedy of the Flying Dutchman?

Those who put a deadline or a scoop ahead of all else must bear some responsibility for the escalation of these grotesque acts of violence. To merely say that "if I don't report it, others will," is tantamount to saying "if I don't steal, others will." Civilized codes of conduct preclude us from the latter—why not from the former?

LET US LOOK at the list of aircraft attractions for terrorists that we have examined so far:

- High cost target—easily destroyed,
- Huge array of hostages and nationalities,
- Ability to attack larger power with little threat to one's own security,
- Enormous publicity worldwide and an ability to move the stage and the act to any audience in the world,

and finally, the very pièce-de-résistance of the target—when the terrorist is ready to ring down the curtain on a particular event—the target can itself provide the means of escape to sanctuary. Just land in Beirut, for example, and melt into the crowd.

Large passenger aircraft are the quintessential target of choice, but as we know from bitter experience, there are many

Target of Choice

other targets. There have been embassies, boats, ships, banks, offices, and even trains but none will ever rival aircraft, for no others have as many attractive features.

5

Horror In the Cabin—A Flight Attendant's Story

"As soon as I recognized the language as Arabic, I knew we were being hijacked." The words came from the elegant, classically beautiful woman who sat near me on the sectional couch in the gracious warmth of her living room.

Even though we had met previously, it was hard to accept that this slight, even delicate person could have endured and prevailed during the days of horror on board TWA 847 that began on June 14, 1985.

Uli Derickson had been the senior flight attendant or purser on that ill-fated flight, a fortuitous assignment as later events were to reveal.

Knowing of my work in the field of antiterrorism in civil aviation, Uli had agreed to an interview, which, as I was to discover, was for her a very painful process of remembering. At the kind invitation of Uli and her husband, retired senior TWA captain, Russell Derickson, I visited their home hidden in the folds of upstate New Jersey's countryside.

The two of us sat in the quiet of her living room, ubiquitous tape recorder on the coffee table and her husband unseen but felt close by as he stayed in earshot ready to lend support and strength, if needed.

Speaking in the wonderfully clear and grammatical English that only educated foreigners seem to be able to effect, she began her story:

"YOU ARE NEVER prepared for something like this. You can only mentally review what you would do if it happened to you, but if it actually happens you have no time to make a conscious decision. Most of the time the decisions are made instinctively."

She made a point of the fact she was fortunate to have received training that was very helpful in the initial period of surprise and shock and that helped to carry her through until she could assess the situation and make some cogent plans.

The aircraft was airborne out of Athens at approximately 10:00 A.M., approximately one hour late as a result of boarding delays caused by the flight being oversold. There were more passengers than seats. This not uncommon occurrence was to have a bizarre effect on the events to follow.

As the aircraft climbed to its cruising altitude on the way to Rome, the seat belt sign was turned off, but Uli decided not to make an announcement drawing the passengers' attention to it. It was to be a short flight with a full load of passengers, and she and her four other flight attendants had to provide break-

Horror in the Cabin—A Flight Attendant's Story

fast service to all; she wanted the passengers to remain seated and keep the aisles clear.

She had her head in the forward closet, retrieving her serving smock from her bag, when she heard the sound of voices raised in anger. At first she thought that the passengers were up and about, unhappy with their seat assignments (smokers in nonsmoking and vice versa, for example), but as the voices came nearer she recognized Arabic and knew immediately and instinctively that she was facing a crisis.

As she straightened up from the closet, she was thrown violently back against the cockpit door, a gun was roughly thrust against her head, and she was conscious of a hand grenade being waved in front of her face.

Her mind racing, she recalled her training "I automatically began to review all that I was taught: delay, delay, delay—I must delay, try to get to talk to them."

One of the two hijackers leaped up in the air and delivered a karate kick with both feet to Uli's left chest, smashing her back into the cockpit door again. The other seized her head and repeatedly beat it against the cockpit door while screaming imprecations at her. *It was a classic move of lots of violent, nonlethal blows combined with a loud verbal assault intended to gain control and subdue resistance immediately.* This maneuver is taught to law-enforcement and military special forces the world over.

Uli had lived in Saudi Arabia for two years and had a rough but working understanding of Arabic. She could speak a little and understand more. As the beating and shouting continued, she realized that the foul language was being directed against "the Americans." She stopped the two terrorists dead in their tracks by telling them in Arabic that she was German and perhaps she could help them.

They were so astonished that they immediately stopped their assault and looked at her. One of the terrorists then spoke to her in perfect, flawless, but heavily accented German.

Uli reacted in surprise, "My God, I thought, who am I dealing with?"

Now having established communication with one of them, she began to work at building a rapport. The German-speaking terrorist stopped the other from continuing the beating, which he had begun again following his initial surprise at Uli's use of Arabic. He, it turned out, could speak a few rehearsed English sentences but no language other than Arabic.

"Just a minute," cried the first terrorist. "She is from Germany, wait a minute," while the other began beating on the cockpit door screaming in English, "Open the door" over and over again.

After delaying them for several more minutes, Uli was obliged to get the key to the door from her purse to prevent them from trying to shoot the lock off.

It was at this point in her story that Uli mentioned one of her more chilling observations. Both terrorists were obviously highly trained in applying *psychological terrorism* but were woefully ignorant of any technical aspects of flying. Having gained access to the cockpit, they were confronted with two pilots seated forward and facing forward and one seated behind and sideways to them at the flight engineer instrument panel.

They began beating on the co-pilot Phil Maresca in the mistaken belief that he was the captain. Here again, there was physical and verbal assault in an effort to intimidate and

Horror in the Cabin—A Flight Attendant's Story

control immediately. Their complete lack of technical aviation knowledge was later and further revealed in their initial inability to use the radio hand microphone and the demands for flights to destinations way beyond the maximum range of the aircraft.

Uli also noted that they were both extremely nervous about flying, for they became quite perturbed when some light turbulence was encountered later in the flight and she found herself in the bizarre position of having to comfort and calm them! She knew that she had to keep them as stable as possible.

The one item they seemed to know about was the crash ax always kept in the cockpit. The flight engineer, Christian Zimmermann, had cleverly and quickly concealed it as the terrorists were trying to gain access to the cockpit. They asked for it, drew pictures of it, but when the crew convincingly acted out ignorance they dropped the matter.

Because Uli spoke both German and English she became the sole communications link between the terrorists and their captives. In later conversations she discovered that the German-speaking terrorist, whom the crew named Castro (the other was called Said, as in Port Said), had lived in Germany with a German common-law wife.

This ability to communicate was unquestionably the single most important element in the survival of the crew and passengers of flight 847, for what was not known in the beginning was that a third terrorist was to have boarded in Athens. He evidently was English-speaking and was the leader of the group and possessor of the plan. He failed to board the flight *because he arrived too late to get a seat assignment and it was oversold.*

The irony of this situation is almost unbearable. Because of his absence his henchmen were unable to communicate with their victims, had little idea of the plans for the flight following the plane's seizure, and had to improvise in a highly volatile situation without the benefit of their cell leader.

But for the fortuitous and one might say, God-given, presence of Arabic-German-English-speaking Uli Derickson, total disaster would have been almost certain. In many ways the lives of those 145 passengers and eight crew members lay in the hands of a slightly built young woman who out of uniform could be mistaken for a fashion model from the pages of *Vogue*. *She provided a means of communication.*

To illustrate the importance of communications in these situations, at one point in the flight Castro wanted one male passenger to get up from his seat. He commanded him, "Sit down! Sit down!" The bewildered fellow scrunched down further in his seat. Furiously, Castro began pistol-whipping him. "Sit down! Sit down!" Uli was able to get to him before he killed the passenger and explained that he was using the wrong English phrase and, indeed, was telling the man to do the opposite of what he wanted him to do.

In addition to providing a language communications link with the terrorists, Uli was able to provide another link that was also very important. Because of her time in Saudi Arabia she had become familiar with Arabic culture. In conversations with Castro, it became clear that some very deep, personal grievances burned deep within him. Uli reported, "The Arabic people, especially Palestinians, are very sensitive. They are convinced that Americans view them as idiots, as third-class citizens. That came out very early in the conversations. They are tired of being treated like animals—they are human beings like we are." She went on to advise, "If we can view them, despite all our fears, as humans," and she hastened to add that such a view has nothing to do with the Stockholm Syndrome,* "then one can adopt a sympathetic, nonthreatening attitude toward them."

As to the Stockholm Syndrome itself, she was quick to agree that it did take place to a degree and, indeed, it helped keep the situation under control. It seemed that it also worked on the terrorists, for she went on to say; "At one stage during the second flight between Algeria and Beirut, during the four and a half hour night flight, I found a few quiet moments to talk with Castro." Instinctively recognizing the necessity to strengthen the bond that was growing between them due to her unique role of being the sole means of communication, Uli began talking with him of his childhood as a refugee in a Palestinian camp and related that she too was a refugee, having twice escaped from communism to find a new home in the United States. "I told him there are many people on this aircraft with similar backgrounds and that America is made up of people like us, ethnic groups seeking a better life and now you want to kill us." He seemed surprised that she was an American and asked, "Are you sure?" and Uli responded that, indeed, she was.

The conversation then edged into the dangerous area of religion, but once again Uli's international background and education stood her in good stead for she was able to discuss the Koran with some degree of knowledge and understanding.

Having this terrorist, armed with a handgun and grenades,

---

*See page 109 for an explanation of the Stockholm Syndrome.

calmed down to the point where he began to question his actions was a remarkable accomplishment. Castro astonished Uli by quietly asking her if she could sing. "Thinking that I would try anything at this stage, I told him yes, and he asked me to sing a specific song, 'Patty-cake, Patty-cake,' in German." This told Uli that Castro at least at one time had a child or a family. As it turned out, he had a child by his German girlfriend. It is probable that missing his child and the child's mother, he was engaging in some identity transfer with Uli.

"When I sang" Uli said, "his eyes filled with tears." Facing a human being about to kill, she thought, "If I can only handle this right, we can get out of this alive."

One must understand that through this entire ordeal, with few exceptions, Uli was the only one permitted to move about and talk. For days the other flight attendants were forced to sit on the floor of the aft gallery or on their jump seats. The pilots had to remain seated in the cockpit, and the passengers were obliged to remain seated with their heads down below seatback level, a cruel position for the infirm and elderly who were obliged to maintain that posture for endless hours.

"It was the most eerie feeling," Uli said, "to look back into a cabin that you know contains over a hundred forty passengers and not be able to see them."

Throughout the ordeal the hijackers kept moving people around like pawns in a chess game. Their intent was as obvious as it was clever: it lowered the chances of groups being formed among the passengers that could pose a threat to them. Able-bodied men were made to sit in window seats with women and children occupying aisle or center seats, blocking the men from quick access to the aisle. This was particularly unfortu-

Horror in the Cabin—A Flight Attendant's Story

nate for those occupying the aisle seats, for the terrorists, again following training for psychological control by terror, constantly beat and assaulted those passengers within reach. With their hands, pistols, and grenades they beat women and children without discrimination.

Uli reported that at one time she was seated in a jump seat right at the class divider separating first-class from coach. The terrorists had moved everyone into the coach section.

An elderly woman in the front row aisle seat, raised her head from the uncomfortable position she had held for hours, presumably to catch a breath of air (it was very hot) or ease her back, when Said, who was walking past, leaped into the air and karate-kicked the woman in the face with both feet, smashing her spectacles into her face. This unremitting imposition of brutal violence and terror continued throughout the entire time that Said and Castro were the only terrorists on board.

Difficult though it was, it was necessary to display some sympathy for the terrorists to keep them as calm as possible. "In my opinion it is necessary," Uli said, "to convince them that you are understanding and cooperative. That does not mean, however, that you should do everything they tell you to. You don't have to roll over for them. There were tasks he wanted me to do, and finally I said this is enough." She continued: "I said, 'We are cooperating, we are doing everything you asked us to do, you promised me over the lips of Allah'—you know how they gesture with the hand from the mouth—and he immediately stopped. They do not like to be shown to be lying by doing something they said they wouldn't." This is how she fought back, quietly using whatever weakness or vulnerabilities she was able to exploit.

None of the hostages were allowed to speak or communicate with each other in any way. Uli, however, was allowed to talk with Castro, but to no one else except to relay instructions. However, one of the terrorists gave her a piece of chewing gum that she chewed on for two entire days—a world record, perhaps? She was able to work her mouth, chewing the gum, and quietly mutter words to passengers and other crew members.

At one stage, three male passengers had developed a plan to jump the terrorists. Uli was able to convey to the three, who were now separated by a couple of rows, that the hand grenades had been confirmed as real by one of the military personnel on board and if they were to try anything, they should do it only on the ground, for she feared the grenades would destroy the aircraft in flight.

Unfortunately, all the time the aircraft was on the ground, the terrorists held the grenades in their hands with the pins pulled. All they would have to do to explode the grenades was to let go of them.

Meanwhile the beatings continued. I asked Uli if she thought the beatings were an expression of anger or frustration or were they initiated as a conscious, trained means of subjugation and control. She replied: "While it was true that they were angry at everyone on the airplane but nobody in particular, it was intended to show the people that they were the boss." She added: "It was a constant up and down situation. For a while I would think they had calmed down, then one would jump up and begin beating on the nearest victim at hand."

Given this bizarre pattern of behavior, I asked if there was any sign that the terrorists were under the influence of drugs. She was quite firm in her answer: "I don't think they were ever on drugs. They were very clearheaded and not under the influence of anything." In the first half hour of the takeover, however, they did exhibit wild behavior, sweating profusely and screaming continuously in English, "We have come to die." This was one English phrase they had rehearsed very well. Uli gave a wry laugh and said: "We did, of course, take them seriously." The intensity of the terrorists' dedication was underscored later when Castro told Uli that it made absolutely no difference to him if he died now or forty years later. He made this clear to Uli and made her make the cockpit crew understand it, too. Several times during the initial hours she literally begged them not to kill the passengers and crew, she was so convinced of their willingness to do so and die with them if necessary.

They tried to convince Uli that there were five of them on board—the other three as "sleepers" among the passengers. This lie soon became apparent for, as Uli reported, "Everyone was so obviously scared to death," so terrified of the terrorists that not one of them could be a collaborator. Uli conveyed this information to the cockpit crew with details of the weapons she had seen.

She came up with an interesting observation when asked how she knew what to say to them to enable her to "contain" the situation and prevent it from escalating into total destruction.

"It was simply a case of never telling them 'yes' or 'no.' If I was to say 'yes' I would commit myself to something and if you say 'no' you get them angry. I tried to equivocate in a reasonable manner."

At one stage they ordered Uli to hand out paper cups of water to the passengers and became upset when it was taking too long for their liking. She asked if she could get the other flight attendants to assist as there were 143 passengers to serve. When that request was denied, she told Castro that if he wanted it done quickly he had better help. Whereupon she handed him a tray of cups and told him to pass them out! Astonished, he did as he was told, gun in one hand, tray in the other.

When she overplayed her "authority" role several times, they threatened to blow her head off. On those occasions she apologized, said she was sorry, and they calmed down.

There were rumors of a sexual assault on one of the flight attendants, which later proved false. Indeed, the terrorists were so fanatically religious that they ordered Uli to use blankets to cover the legs of female passengers who were wearing shorts. They said they were offended by such brazenness. After several hours of denial, passengers were allowed to use the toilets in the rear of the aircraft. The doors remained open but whenever a female used the toilet, Said, who was guarding that area, turned his back so he could not see. Such delicacy from one who had been violently beating the same people was surely confusing to the hostages.

When preparing beverages or food for the terrorists, Uli made sure that they saw everything she did in preparing them. They were obviously alert to the possibility of their food or drink being drugged. It was evident that, except for their lack of aviation knowledge, the terrorists had been well trained. This is important to note, for it indicates a marked increase in sophistication and planning by Arab terrorist groups conspicuously absent in previous incidents.

Horror in the Cabin—A Flight Attendant's Story

During this particular hijacking, a now familiar but chilling event took place: the collection of passports for the purpose of identifying Jews, Israelis, and Americans. It is worthwhile noting that this occurrence on TWA 847 was so badly misreported by the news media that for a while Uli Derickson was accused of selecting the Jews among the passengers. Indeed, *The New York Times* had a front-page story attesting to that "fact." When it became clear that, indeed, Uli had actually concealed the passport of one Jewish passenger and talked the terrorists out of finding the remaining Jews, *The Times* published a correction in a later edition. It was on page 19 and only in the edition distributed in the New York City area.

The passports were collected and dumped into a first-class seat for examination. When told to pick out Israeli passports, Uli replied that there were none. When told to select the Jews, she said: "No way, there is no way of telling as American passports do not show religion" and supported her reply by showing Castro a passport.

"Come with me," he snapped, and pulling out a passenger list that had been taped to the wall of the forward galley, he made Uli read each name one by one. When she came to a name like Rosenblum, she was told to find his passport. The first passport with a Jewish name that she found she concealed in another passport. After going through this exercise of finding a name and then the matching passport seven times, Castro stopped his search as he apparently lost interest in finding more. He next turned his attention to the seven military personnel, whose identities were revealed by the military IDs they carried in lieu of passports, and carefully placed them in widely separated seats throughout the cabin. The same process was used to segregate the seven Jewish passengers, or at least those he thought were Jewish.

When they had completed this task, the terrorists had each of the seven military passengers brought to the first-class section, one at a time, for interrogation. The first was U.S. Navy diver Robert Stethem.

Uli reports that the 23-year-old Stethem was a tall, powerful looking young man. He was brave, and he was proud, and evidently it showed. The two terrorists were small and skinny and apparently viewed Stethem as a potential threat to the hijacking and, perhaps, their own manhood.

Uli, as translator, tried to explain that Stethem was a Navy man, but the German for Navy is Marine and they became excited and angry and kept repeating "Marine, Marine." Uli carefully explained that, no, he was a sailor and not like the U.S. Marines who had been stationed in Beirut.

After the interrogation, Stethem was returned to his seat, and the others were interrogated in turn. Unfortunately for Robert Stethem, his seat was the one closest to the front of the aircraft; the other six military personnel were seated farther back.

On the second stop in Algeria when demands for fuel were being made and not being complied with, the terrorists took Stethem forward and began beating him terribly. It should be noted that he was first restrained by tying his arms and wrists behind him with the rubber cords the flight attendants used to hold their crew bags on the small suitcase carts they use. The bindings were so tight, spitefully so, that all circulation was cut off as the cords bit deeply into his flesh.

Uli described the horror. "He picked this man to come up

Horror in the Cabin—A Flight Attendant's Story

front for the beating simply because he was military and sat the most forward. He had done nothing wrong other than show a little pride." Convinced that they were about to lose their first passenger, for the terrorists were ready to kill to get fuel, Uli intervened, and Stethem was allowed back to his seat, half-carried by Uli. He was half-conscious, bleeding heavily, with one eye out of its socket and his arms totally devoid of any blood because of the tight cords that bound them.

Uli begged the terrorists to let her untie his arms, as he was half dead and posed no threat to them. Eventually, Castro allowed her to untie Stethem's bonds, which took an age for the rubber cords were buried so deeply in his arms.

Prior to and after Stethem's beating the terrorists had cried out in Arabic and English, "One American must die." This was like a mantra for a ritual yet to come. The ritual was played out on the tarmac of Beirut airport a few hours later.

After landing in Beirut, the TWA aircraft taxied past the burned-out wreck of a Royal Jordanian Airlines L-1011 that had been hijacked and blown up on the ground a few days earlier. Uli was instructed to tell the passengers to look out the windows at the wreck, which by then consisted of the tail-plane area only, for that would be what their aircraft would look like if anyone moved or did anything wrong. She conveyed that message to the passengers and added that they would come out alive if she had their total cooperation.

Stethem was then taken from his seat, dragged forward into the first-class section, and shot twice in cold blood. The terrorists opened the forward cabin door, dumped his body onto the ramp, and closed the door. Lending credence to the ritualistic aspect of the killing was Uli's comment: "It was dead silent on the airplane. You could have heard a pin drop. All the window shades were closed—it was pitch dark. I felt my heart beating wildly, for I thought someone may now try to storm the aircraft." To add further to the macabre situation, she went on, "Breaking the silence, one of the two men, I don't know which one it was, began singing a song. I recognized that song as a victory song, for I had heard it before. It was a song of celebration." They also scrawled slogans on the aircraft's doors and bulkheads with Stethem's blood.

Fortunately, the passengers remained calm. It was a highly volatile moment and could have turned into carnage with the slightest spark.

It is worth noting in retrospect that while it is clear that the violence that occurred was undoubtedly intended to subjugate and control, some elements of personal humiliation or revenge crept in. After beating one of the other military passengers, a physically powerful-looking black American, Castro sneered and boasted to Uli, "Look at him, they think they are so big and strong, look how big his muscles are and yet I can beat him." She pointed out that the victim had a gun to his head and was bound with his hands behind his back. "So what," Castro sneered. "Americans are so big and so stupid."

Castro then corrected himself by carefully explaining that he only hated American military personnel and the government. He said over and over that he did not hate the American people, only the American government, its collaboration with Israel, and the military. He kept mentioning New Jersey over and over. Uli almost mentioned that she lived in New Jersey but fortunately she decided that the old military axiom "never volunteer anything or for anything" was a good one, for it turned out that Castro was speaking of the U.S. Navy battleship *New Jersey,* which had shelled Beirut. Castro reminded Uli of a marketplace in a village in the Bekaa Valley where a number of children and sixty women were killed at prayer by a 12-inch shell from the U.S.S. *New Jersey*. He shouted "And you cry about one man dying. Women and children die daily on the streets of Beirut, and nobody cries about them." Getting more excited, he continued: "Your newspapers lie to you, you only hear the Israeli side, you are not informed of what is happening in our country." Uli said he went on and on; this was his main theme, his main grievance. He insisted that Uli carry the message to the American people that if the United States stopped collaborating with Israel half its problems would be over.

On one of the trips from Algeria to Beirut, Castro suddenly jumped up and announced that they were not going to Beirut but were going to Israel and he would blow the plane up over Tel Aviv. Uli reminded him again that, over the lips of Allah, he had promised her that whatever happened, she would get out alive. Still uncertain as to his intentions, she went off to her forward jump seat and quietly cried, prayed, and prepared herself and found what she described as "incredible peace."

During her further, obviously successful attempts to dissuade him from his new goal, she suggested Lybia as an alternative destination. Castro recoiled in horror at the thought of getting involved with that "crazy man Quaddafi." He asserted that Quaddafi "does not believe in Allah" and went on about how wonderful the Ayatollah Khomeini is and that he is the true leader of Islam. He displayed an extensive knowledge of his religion and obviously had complete faith in it. While speaking of religion, Uli remarked that it was her Catholic faith that sustained her. "I can assure you, Tom," she said, "there was not an atheist on that airplane."

Because of her experience in early life in escaping from Czechoslovakia to East Germany and then later from East Germany to West Germany, Uli had developed a knowledge of handguns. At some point on one of the interminable flights, she picked up Castro's handgun, which was on a seat between them. He watched her pick it up as, feigning curiosity, she tried to figure out how to cock it for firing. She could tell it was an automatic with the safety catch on (revolvers do not have safety catches), but she was unable to figure out how to prepare it for firing. "It was a beautifully crafted Spanish-made automatic with real mother-of-pearl handle grips, and I held his gun pretending to admire it." Castro suddenly leaped to his feet, snatched the gun from her hand, ran back into the coach cabin, screamed some obscenities at the passengers and then returned. As things turned out it was probably just as well that Uli did not try to kill him.

On the second landing in Beirut, a group of Shiite militia got on board. They appeared to be from two groups, the Ahmal and the Hezbollah. The Ahmal seemed quite disciplined and had with them an English-speaking man in a smart business suit who announced to the passengers that no one was going to kill them. He was very reassuring, and the increase in the number of Arabic hostage takers seemed to relax the atmosphere considerably. Said and Castro were now effectively replaced by militia, and the strain of command and planning was lifted from their shoulders. Many of the newcomers spoke good English. One confessed to Uli that he was a schoolteacher.

Horror in the Cabin—A Flight Attendant's Story

However, a few among the Hezbollah group were little more than young, armed thugs who looted money and jewelry from the passengers. Castro expressed both his disgust and disdain for those individuals and would have nothing to do with them. At the time in Beirut when the first batch of women and children hostages were released, Uli stood at the top of the slide directing them when it crossed her mind that she had only to step forward and she too would be free. Perhaps sensing her thoughts, Castro stepped up to her and told her, "Not you, not now." He still needed her presence, and she knew that she was needed by the passengers so she elected to stay.

Toward the end of the ordeal for Uli and the remaining women and children, she was told that she would be released in Beirut. This was stopped by one of the Ahmal who said "No! Where would you go, Beirut is a city at war. It's better to stay with us."

On the last trip to Algiers for Uli, Castro told her that when Ali Attwa (the third terrorist who failed to board in Athens) arrived in Algiers from Athens where he had been arrested, she would be released. Ali Attwa was flown to Algeria on Olympic Airlines and eventually was allowed to join his companions. While awaiting his arrival, Uli was allowed to leave via the aft stairs. She donned her uniform jacket and walked down the stairs. At the bottom she encountered an English-speaking Shiite militiaman, and she said to him that surely Ali Attwa was worth the exchange of more than one woman. "How about releasing the rest of my crew?" she boldly asked. The militiaman left her under the gun of his companion, boarded the aircraft for a few minutes, came back down, and told Uli to re-embark!

When back on board, she was told that when Ali Attwa actually arrived, she and her cabin crew would be released. Uli's negotiations cost her another eight hours of captivity.

Finally Attwa arrived, and Castro told Uli, "You and your crew *and* ten women may get off, for Ali Attwa is worth that many." As Uli was leaving she noticed that one of those being released was a young sub-teenage girl. She asked Castro if he would let her mother go with her. At first he said no, but, after pleading that it was dangerous to let a young girl free into a strange country, Uli finally convinced him to let her mother go with her.

The aircraft then returned to Beirut with terrorists, militia, cockpit crew, and the remaining hostages. After the hostages were dispersed to secret locations in Beirut, almost two more weeks passed before their release was negotiated.

Several weeks later, the filthy, battered but still airworthy Boeing 727 was flown to Cyprus and thence to the United States for refurbishing and major overhaul.

The greatest aviation terrorist saga finally came to an end. There were many heros and villains. Other than the terrorists themselves, the next greatest villains were those in the news media, particularly from the United States. The Algerians also qualify by their lack of support and assistance to U.S. needs. There is little doubt that specially trained forces could have taken that aircraft on the ground with little or no loss of life. It must be remembered that the threat was total destruction, and there was every reason to believe it.

Castro, Said, and Attwa disappeared into the bedlam and hell of Beirut and Lebanon, prices on their heads, hunted men.

Robert Stethem died a brave man and a proud American,

little solace perhaps for his family and friends. The rest of the hostages went their ways, some, if not all, to fall prey to that other school of sharks in our society, the lawyers who doubtless will begin multiple law suits against everyone.

The crew of TWA 847 were Captain John Testrake, First Officer Phil Maresca, Second Officer Christian Zimmermann, the flight attendants Hazel Hesp, Elizabeth Howes, Judy Cox, Helen Sheahan, and, of course, the hero of them all—Uli Derickson—who at the end had this to say about her tormentors: "If they are captured I will, of course, be a witness at their trial, and I have pondered this thought all the time since it happened—what will I do? Do I have any feelings of revenge? Yes and no—I'm torn. They must be brought to justice, for they committed murder and they brutalized an airplane full of people. That's an intellectual response. Emotionally, I feel something for them, I feel for their people, where they come from, those I have compassion for. So I am torn."

Several weeks after the incident, Uli had her Shell Oil credit card returned to her from the refueler in Beirut who had insisted on payment of some kind before he would gas the aircraft. TWA paid the $12,500.00 billed to her account.

6

An Ounce of Prevention

Almost all airline pilots in the United States belong to the Air Line Pilots Association. Founded in 1932 to counter the dreadful lack of aviation safety, it continues to this day to be the main spokesman, research source, and last line of defense for the air traveler.

Since its early beginnings it has grown into a large, highly sophisticated organization, part professional association and part labor union. There is little question that many of the innovations that have enhanced the safety of air travel came from the multitude of technically expert committees and research programs of the Air Line Pilots Association. Its Engineering and Air Safety Department and its Accident Investigation Department are recognized worldwide as being second to none.

Beginning in the late sixties and really taking off in 1971, the Air Line Pilots Association began an intense, methodical program to find adequate defenses against hijackings.

Several basic parameters were set within which a detailed operational plan would be devised. The pilot committee charged with this task determined from the outset that they did not want crew members armed. Pilot crew members' primary duty was to fly the aircraft, and the danger of losing one or all of them in a firefight was too great a risk. As to arming flight attendants, the idea of a shoot-out in a pressurized aircraft at 30,000 feet was also too horrible to contemplate.

Unlike what much fiction would have you believe, a bullet hole in the wall of the cabin is not going to suddenly expand and grow into a gaping hole through which the contents of the cabin would disappear in a roaring rush of air. However, other than as a threat to people, a bullet can smash through or into any of the hundreds of electronic, hydraulic, fuel, electrical, and manual systems and controls that keep the aircraft flying.

Concealed behind wall panels and below floors, these pipes, wires, black boxes, and cables are the life system of an aircraft. Just like the life system in your body, the aircraft has a heart, arteries, muscle, and sinew, and continuing the analogy, while most of them can suffer some degree of trauma, there are vital parts and organs that are necessary to sustain life.

Aircraft manufacturers realize this of course as do the government agencies that certify an aircraft as being airworthy. To this end, the essential fuel, hydraulic, electrical and electronic systems are duplicated, triplicated, and, in some cases, quadrupled to provide for backup in case of failure or destruction of a system or systems.

However, pilots—like most people—would prefer their aircraft not to be shot at even in nonfatal places; hence, our rejection of guns on board our aircraft. In brief, pilots believe that there are no "good" guns or "bad" guns. A gun can pass from good to bad by changing hands. When a hijacker has a hostage with a gun or knife at the hostage's throat, the threat to the hostage's life is usually sufficient to persuade people to give up whatever other weapons are known to be on board and add them to the hijacker's arsenal.

For a short time in the early 1970s, armed sky marshals were, by Presidential Executive Order, placed on U.S. air carrier flights. These much ballyhooed and overpublicized individuals were close to being as great a danger to civil aviation as those they were meant to protect us against.

Sparsely trained, overused, underqualified, and improperly armed, these "shot-gun riders" had a thankfully brief existence. Passengers would play "spot the sky-marshal" games in flight. It was an easy game, for all one had to ascertain was who was the passenger who didn't drink alcohol, take off his jacket, watch the movie, or listen to the stereo. He was also the one who carefully watched each passenger who went forward to the front toilets near the cockpit.

The ineffectiveness of the program was illustrated when in 1971 an American Airlines Boeing 747 with three sky marshals on board was hijacked to Cuba by a man whose weapon turned out to be a ballpoint pen!

The airline pilots of the United States rose up in anger at this dangerous appendage to an already complicated and sometimes hazardous condition, and that ill-conceived, though well-intentioned program was allowed to die away.

The greatest fear of the pilots' security experts was that the public acceptance of the glamorous portrayal of these sky marshals would take the pressure off the airlines, government, and regulatory agencies to develop and institute an effective system of *pre-board screening*. The Air Line Pilots Association had determined that prevention was better than cure and that a gun discovered prior to boarding was preferable to one discovered afterward. In short, if one dollar was to be spent on aircraft security, we wanted all one hundred cents of it to go for preemptive and preventative activities. In the end we prevailed, and in 1974 the Anti-Hijacking bill was signed by President Nixon and 100 percent pre-board screening passed into the lexicon of aviation terms.

While all this activity was going on in the United States, the pilots of the world, spearheaded by U.S. pilots, were making great attempts to introduce similar protection throughout the world's airports and at the same time began seeking new protocols to ensure the swift, severe punishment of hijackers either by the country in which they were captured or in that which they were extradicted to.

To dramatize their demands, the world's pilots through their international organization of the International Air Line Pilots Associations (IFALPA) on June 19, 1974 called for a worldwide twenty-four-hour suspension of service. The action was generally well supported in those countries where free trade unionism was recognized, and even some countries less liberal in their labor policies permitted their pilots to support the shutdown. In the United States the trade association of the airlines, the Air Transport Association (ATA), took legal action against the pilots and obtained restraining orders against a number of pilots in leadership positions. I recall hiding out from the sheriffs and marshals in a motel in Westbury, Long Island, with three of my cohorts. Coincident with the release of the hit movie *The Godfather,* we referred to it as "hitting the mattresses."

My job was coordinating with all the foreign pilot groups throughout the world. During a forty-eight hour period I made about a hundred telephone calls to about forty foreign capital cities. The calls were made through the motel switchboard operator. I remember when the operation was over and we were checking out of the motel, curiosity overcame fear and the motel manager asked us who we were. When we revealed our identity, he confessed that the motel staff had after much discussion concluded that we were part of some huge international gambling consortium!

In a way I guess we were gamblers; the effort to shut down the United States was only partially successful inasmuch as many groups of airline pilots went to work under court orders and a few failed to give any support to the effort. Insofar as it was not a win, it at least could be characterized as a "place," for we had created sufficient turmoil to get attention, and the United Nations and various important civil aviation nations finally began to lumber into action.

To national and international bodies accustomed to moving at glacial speed, the moves to provide 100 percent pre-board screening of all passengers boarding U.S. carriers at both national and overseas airports caught them by surprise. Countries that had yet to introduce any security screening for flights on their own national carriers began to make some incremental moves toward passenger screening. Some hard checking of carry-on baggage was conducted, a few metal detectors were purchased, and in one or two countries, a 10 percent random checking system was introduced—that is, screening on only 10 percent of their flights. The pace quickened when passengers began moving from their own unchecked national airlines flights onto security-screened U.S. flights, and security became an obvious though unmentioned factor in airline marketing.

Still, throughout all this time, the term "terrorist" had yet to be applied and "hijacker" was the standard term.

THE INCREASING DIFFICULTY or even inability to get weapons on board aircraft by passengers then created the paradox of even more dangerous forms of attack. The result of this was the increase in sabotage and sabotage attempts.

In the years 1949 through 1984 there have been eighty explosions on board aircraft, killing a total of 1,149. The bulk of deaths and incidents of sabotage increased dramatically after 1974. Now the civil aviation industry had to deal with this even more difficult specter.

A curiosity of the number of bombings on planes is that, unlike other forms of attacks on civil aviation, the bombings have not been concentrated against U.S. airlines. The victim aircraft have been from countries of registry from all over the world. Airlines as disparate as Aeroflot (USSR) and Air Vietnam (South Vietnam) have fallen to saboteurs, and the motives for such crimes have been equally disparate.

A number of bombings have been attributed to attempts to collect insurance on one of the victims. For a few dollars paid at a convenient flight insurance booth or automatic policy-issue machine right at the airport, one may cover the insured for hundreds of thousands of dollars. A number of people have loaded a spouse on board an aircraft with an explosive device tucked away in the spouse's suitcase so thoughtfully packed by the other. One can never really be certain of the real number of such events or attempts, for not all come to light due to the disappearance at sea of the wreckage or the failure of devices to explode and the seemingly innocent package delivered intact to its apparent destination.

The most notorious of known incidents occurred on June 15, 1972. A Cathay Pacific Convair 880 enroute from Bangkok to Hong Kong was blown from the skies over the central highlands of South Vietnam. There were no survivors, and eighty-one crew and passengers died. The perpetrator had figured out the timing very well and was banking on authorities being unable to get to any wreckage because of the wild terrain and the fact that a full-scale war was in progress in that area.

He had not figured on the tenacity of the U.S. National Transportation Safety Board (N.T.S.B.), which had been called in to assist in the investigation. Investigator-in-Charge Doug Dreifyus is a dogged, complete professional with a deep personal commitment to find out "why?" to prevent a recurrence. I was to get to know Doug very well later on.

Based upon clues yielded by a thorough examination of the wreckage, it was ascertained that a bomb had exploded under a passenger seat on the right side of the aircraft over the wing. A check back in Bangkok revealed that among the passengers in the immediate vicinity of the explosion was a young woman seen on board by a senior police officer from Bangkok. Witnesses recalled him giving her a suitcase to take with her just before take off. Forensic evidence indicated it was that suitcase that held the bomb. He was charged, found guilty, and executed.

AT ALMOST THE same time as I first became involved in aviation security, I undertook a course of training in aircraft accident investigation, for I felt, unhappily, that both disciplines would soon be needed in conjunction with each other.

One of the things I learned was the extraordinary talent and dedication of many of the field investigators of the N.T.S.B. Their reputation is such that worldwide they are invited and, indeed, cajoled into involvement in investigations of aircraft accidents of foreign airlines in foreign countries.

The painstaking investigative procedures are extraordinary, and their ability to produce actual evidence of probable cause is nothing short of amazing. The actual findings are made and issued by the National Transportation Safety Board itself, which consists of political appointees, a fact that frequently becomes apparent in some of its decisions and utterances. The field investigators can only provide evidence; they cannot issue a probable cause.

I came to admire the outstanding work of these people but always under the saddest of circumstances. I knew of Doug Dreifyus's reputation long before death and destruction brought us together in September 1974.

IT WAS A bright clear day over the Ionian Sea as the Pan American Boeing 747 headed eastbound out of Rome en route along the airways to Beirut at a flight level of 33,000 feet. The general direction of the airway would take the jumbo jet south of Greece.

An Ounce of Prevention

In the cockpit the pilots went about their tasks, keeping a sharp lookout for other aircraft; radar was notoriously poor in this area. Looking out of the left cockpit window the Pan Am captain noticed another aircraft on a reciprocal heading slightly ahead and below him. As he watched, the aircraft, which he could now see was a red and white TWA Boeing 707, suddenly pitched nose up and began a steep climb through the flight level of the Pan Am flight.

With growing horror, the Pan Am captain watched as the 707's pitch grew steeper, way beyond any operational angle permissible for a transport aircraft. Due to the rapid closure rate between the two aircraft, the captain found he had to turn his head far to the left to follow the plane for he had passed the aircraft, which was now falling over the top of its steep climb and entering a steep, downward spiral.

So astonished at witnessing a large jetliner performing an aerobatic maneuver, the captain allowed the autopilot to keep him traveling farther from the stricken aircraft's earthward path. By the time the realization of what he had seen had sunk in, he had lost the aircraft from sight. The whole episode had taken a few, brief seconds.

He quickly radioed to the Athens Flight Information Region, whose control area he was within, and reported the astonishing sight he had just witnessed. He continued to his destination after providing as much information as he was able to remember. Later, under hypnosis, he recalled seeing the aircraft pass through a number of pieces of shiny material fluttering down toward the sea below.

Search and rescue facilities were immediately alerted and dispatched to the area. The U.S.A.F. maintained an airbase at

Athens airport, and U.S. Air Force personnel were scrambled to assist. Some ships of the U.S. Navy Sixth Fleet, present in the Mediterranean, began steaming toward the crash area.

When confirmation came that the aircraft was missing and presumed down in the sea, various people in the United States began quickly packing suitcases and making rapid travel plans. Field investigators of the N.T.S.B., officials from TWA, the Boeing Aircraft Company, Pratt and Whitney (the engine manufacturers), and me, representing the Air Line Pilots Association, began the long, sad trip from the United States to Athens, Greece.

While we were winging our way eastward, ships of the Sixth Fleet and other surface and aircraft were scouring the area of presumed crash. The seas were mercifully calm, and the weather provided excellent searching conditions. From U.S. airbases in England, officials rushed special equipment to detect the signals from a transmitter located in the aircraft's flight data recorder (the famous, but misnamed, black box of news media note), which is designed to begin automatic transmission upon impact. All possible resources, local, American, and others, were utilized and swung into action.

Ships of the Sixth Fleet began picking up bodies and debris from the sea. In one macabre case the bodies of three Japanese passengers still strapped into a row of seats was recovered from the sea. Of the eight-eight crew and passengers, twenty-one bodies were recovered. Along with the bodies were parts of the aircraft's rudder assembly and cabin and cargo compartments. A mass of broken luggage and clothing spread over a wide area. Every piece was picked up to be examined later for any clue that might lead to discovery of what had caused the tragedy.

An Ounce of Prevention

FEARFUL OF THE possibility of sabotage, we, the N.T.S.B. Investigation Team, began assembling in Athens. Using a U.S.A.F. aircraft hangar on the military side of Athens airport, all parts and debris from the crash area were laid out in approximate position relative to the original aircraft structure.

In addition to such physical evidence, many other circumstances were investigated. At one point, I stumbled across a possible cause that later showed a bizarre situation unrelated to the crash but of enormous potential for tragedy. We reasoned that it was entirely possible that another aircraft may have struck the tail plane of the TWA Boeing 707, causing it to lose control. I began checking all air traffic movements in the area.

Airliners fly on airways in the sky just as cars travel on highways on the ground. Over and near land, their progress, position, altitude, and separation from each other is maintained and monitored by ground radar. Over oceans and deserts, where radar does not cover, strict adherence to navigation and on-time arrival at checkpoints is essential for the safe conduct of flight along these busy airways. Because of the lack of radar, aircraft traveling these types of airways must check in with air traffic control at certain prescribed checkpoints with their time at the checkpoint, altitude, speed, and estimated time at the next checkpoint. Air traffic control then keeps a running position of where all the aircraft in their sector are and by voice commands over the radio ensures that separation from other flights is maintained.

By backtracking the reports of an Aeroflot flight out of Damascus to Albania and positioning his speed and reported times on an aeronautical map, I placed him in the vicinity of the doomed TWA flight. The map I was using was an airways map that shows all the airways and checkpoints. Because from time to time airways and checkpoints and other data changes, the maps are renewed and reissued every month or so, and pilots and airlines must maintain complete sets of up-to-date maps or charts.

By plotting the Russian aircraft's position on my chart at the times he had reported, it became clear that his aircraft seemed to be alternately flying at 100 knots per hour for one leg to one checkpoint, then at 900 knots to the next, and so forth. This was very puzzling until a Greek air traffic controller saw something familiar with the position of the checkpoints I had calculated he was inaccurately calling in on. Digging back through the files he found an aeronautical map of the Mediterranean that was several years old. Transposing the Aeroflot positions to that old map showed beyond doubt that its crew had been using a map several years out of date and had presumably been reporting incorrect positions for years! It was a miracle that a collision had not occurred before. The Soviet aviation authorities were informed, but to this day, to my knowledge, no response has been forthcoming. I believe, and pray, they now keep current maps on their aircraft.

HAVING EXHAUSTED THE possibility of a mid-air collision, I joined the army of investigators scrutinizing the wreckage and debris in the hangar. Autopsies of the victims who had been recovered showed they were alive on impact with the sea. Incidentally, hitting water at two- or three-hundred miles an hour is the same as hitting concrete. They all had died of massive crash trauma, spines broken by shear force consistent with a sudden and massive deceleration while restrained by seat belts. This still did not give us any clues to the crash however.

Doug Dreifyus, Investigator-in-Charge (I.I.C.) ordered every piece of nonmetallic debris X-rayed. It was here we got our first clue. We had the lid of a ladies' Samsonite suitcase. A bright pink, it consisted of a thin layer of foam plastic sandwiched between an outer and inner layer of vinyl. There was a small L-shaped tear in the outer skin, and buried in the foam layer, which was only about 1/32 inch thick, was a tiny speck of metal, which had caused the tear and had traveled almost horizontally through the foam layer, a distance of about 1¾ inches. The piece of metal was no bigger than the period at the end of this sentence.

The velocity needed to drive a speck of that weight through the skin and foam of the suitcase lid required an acceleration far greater than the crash could have produced.

Under supermagnification, the metal particle revealed an "orange peel" effect on its surface. This is typically characteristic of metal shrapnel emanating from an explosion.

Spurred by this discovery, more and more X rays were taken and revealed other, larger particles buried in the flooring panels that had been recovered. The flooring was a hard, composite foam sandwiched between aluminum sheets. The greatest concentration of particles was found in the floor section that would also serve as part of the ceiling for the aft cargo hold. Just above that cargo ceiling or below the cabin floor, run the control cables for the rudder and tail plane. Bingo!—we had the cause or at least a preliminary one, which was later confirmed by further forensic evidence and intelligence.

INTELLIGENCE SOURCES BEGAN picking up some clues. Exactly one week earlier, the same flight from Athens to Rome had landed in Rome with a fire in its aft cargo hold. The airport fire department extinguished the blaze and U.S. authorities had shipped the soggy, charred mass to the FBI laboratory in Washington, D.C., for analysis. Word came back by cable; the fire was caused by an incendiary device that had partially malfunctioned due to lack of oxygen in the aft cargo hold in flight (that hold is only partially pressurized).

A young man with Arabic features had traveled on that flight using a South American passport (I believe it was a phony Chilean passport). He disappeared in Rome, and no record of his leaving the country that week could be found. However, he did leave, as a trace of him was found back in Athens at the King Minos Hotel where he had stayed the night before the TWA tragedy. He had shared the room with an older man of Arabic appearance. He boarded the TWA flight for the second time in one week: this time was to be the last flight for him and eighty-seven others.

As best I know, this is the only recorded case of a suicide mission that was carried out twice. He had concealed an explosive device, this time in a backpack he checked at the ticket counter, and got on the flight to certain death. He was a seventeen-year-old Palestinian born and raised in the squalor and hatred of a refugee camp. His companion at the King Minos Hotel was his control; he escaped without a trace.

MOST OF THE defenses that have been installed to protect against sabotage are covert in nature and, therefore, cannot be discussed openly, but there are a number of devices and methods that are openly used and are very effective.

Among those passengers who would give it a thought, most, if not all, would assume that the cargo compartments on passenger jets are filled almost exclusively with baggage belonging to the passengers on board. Indeed, such baggage does occupy a large amount of space, but a surprising amount of airfreight is also carried on passenger flights. Of course, there are a number of airlines that specialize solely in the air shipment of freight. Flying Tigers is the most dominant airfreight carrier, but all passenger aircraft ship hundreds of thousands of tons of freight a day.

On long-haul flights, such as from the United States to Australia for example, it is axiomatic that a full freight compartment will pay the cost of the flight with the passengers on board as "economic gravy." These tons of freight can range in size and weight from an overnight courier packet of a few ounces all the way up to heavy machinery weighing several tons and as huge as automobiles. Frequently the item to be shipped is concealed in its packaging and its contents anonymous, at least to the eye.

Because of their sensitivity to sabotage, U.S. airlines have established a method to avoid the introduction of bombs on board by means of airfreight. Packages accepted for shipping have to come from known certified freight shippers or forwarders who attest in writing to the contents of such packages. Sometimes the package is X-rayed or opened; always, of course, when an unknown or noncertificated shipper or forwarder is involved.

If intelligence warnings indicate a high risk or if there is no urgency for delivery, freight is stored for twenty-four hours prior to being airlifted. As most fuses used in bombs are clockwork, this is one method of ensuring that any clockwork fuse has at least one chance (in the case of a twenty-four-hour watch or clock), and usually two chances, to set off any bomb in the relatively harmless environment of a warehouse.

On flights considered to be high-risk flights, an additional check is made in a barometric chamber. This is a metal chamber the size of a small room that can be pressurized or depressurized to duplicate flight conditions exactly like those experienced in the cargo hold of an aircraft in flight. This is intended to guard against a device known as a barometric fuse, which initiates the chain of events leading to an explosion by the effect of climbing to altitudes or descending from altitudes.

These methods will detect before flight the presence of explosives or incendiary devices in freight except for any that may be using highly sophisticated, esoteric devices, which are extremely difficult to obtain or manufacture. They are also classified and for that and other reasons that should be obvious cannot be discussed or described.

All explosive devices or bombs, if you prefer, have three components. It's no matter if you go from the classic cartoon round bomb with a hissing fuse to an atomic or nuclear device. One needs a power source, an initiator, and an explosive or fissionable substance. In all cases, some sort of timing device is used. Take the cartoon bomb, for example. The hand that strikes the match to light the fuse is the power source. The fuse, by varying its length, is a timing device. As dynamite will not necessarily explode when banged or heated, one needs a small explosion to initiate the larger one. This is accomplished by a blasting cap—the initiator. In various guises such as batteries and clocks, barometrics, and other timing devices, all bombs have the same characteristics.

The most common form of explosive is dynamite. Dynamite is nothing more than nitroglycerine mixed with wax and sawdust or other inert materials and rolled into sticks and wrapped. Now it stands to reason that if one were able to find a means of detecting the chemical elements of nitroglycerine (also present in C4 or plastique) then one would have the basis for an effective explosive-detection device. The theory of explosive-detection devices is well known, and two main means of detection have been discovered. They are known as vapor detection and thermal neutron.

VAPOR DETECTION

Currently, vapor detection is the only known method for screening people for the presence of explosives concealed on them. Because all explosives give off a vapor that is almost impossible to seal in, a means can be found to detect the presence of that vapor. This is called a chemiluminescent process, and it works because of two characteristics of explosives:

1) Such vapors are "sticky" and adhere to metal surfaces much more readily than other effluents; and
2) In a chemiluminescent reaction, the nitric oxide produced by effluent decomposition is mixed with ozone, and a measurable reaction is obtained.

In essence, the air around you, your baggage, or package will be sniffed or sampled to check for the aforementioned reaction. Successful experiments have been conducted with explosives carefully sealed in plastic and other airtight methods of concealment.

THERMAL NEUTRON

Much of the material related to this method is classified, but it can be revealed that the neutrons in any type of explosive can be "excited" by bombarding it with either radioisotopic or electrical "energy" beams. The excitation created is distinctive for all types of explosives and is detectable by sensitive instruments. These methods of detection have been known for many years. The problem has been to adapt the processes, successfully developed and performed under laboratory conditions, and make them work under what must be everyday, practical airport operations conditions.

Ideally, such detection devices would work for both passengers and baggage. Before boarding a flight, a passenger would be obliged to pass through an explosive detection device much like the current magnetometers or metal detectors one sees at all security checkpoints today. Carry-on luggage would also be subjected to the same type of screening in addition to, or in conjunction with, the low-pulse X ray that is currently standard at all U.S. airports. Obviously such methods would be enormously desirable, but for the best security, checked baggage would also undergo rigorous checking.

Let's examine the magnitude of the problem we are dealing with. In the United States alone, U.S. airlines board approximately one billion passengers a year. This in turn translates to about 1.5 billion pieces of hand baggage to be examined, and approximately 2 billion pieces of checked baggage are fed into the cargo holds of the fleet.

Again, when talking about large numbers we have to slow down and get a grasp on what they really look like. Imagine the familiar scene of a sports stadium during the World Series or Super Bowl: the television shots from the Goodyear blimp, the camera passing around the crowded arena; standing room only. Now imagine handling that crowd of people through only one-fourth of the stadium's entrance doors, each fan being checked for possession of weapons or bombs; each fan carrying one bag that must also be similarly checked; and each fan depositing two packed, locked suitcases that are to be transported and stacked under the seats they are to sit in.

On an average, that standing-room-only crowd is about 65,000 people. It would take 15 such stadiums to produce just one million fans. To get a billion fans one would need 1,500 such stadiums filled to capacity. Now we can have some grasp of what one billion passengers look like. Now lets take those billion plus people as the FAA's Office of Civil Aviation Security had to in 1985 and contemplate the following:

Through December 1985, a total of 2,987 firearms were detected at U.S. airport security checkpoints. 2,823 were handguns, 90 were long guns, 74 were firearms that fit neither generic description, being some kind of hybrid, and, in addition, 12 explosive or incendiary devices were discovered. One has to take into account that pre-board screening has been in place for more than ten years, and it was during this time that each and every one of these weapons were detected. Given the wide publicity of the installation of pre-board security checks for passengers and the obvious existence of such checkpoints, one may assume that most, if not all, of these weapons were carried through screening with intent to conceal them from detection. If one carries that assumption even further and accepts that at least 10 percent of such weapons were intended to be used in a hijacking, then it may be claimed that 180 such hijackings were prevented. My personal instinct and experience would put the percentage much higher.

Every so often I can't help wishing that in their thirst for news, our fourth estate could bring themselves to report some good news such as the foregoing statistics. Perhaps, wide publicity would deter many potential hijackers or terrorists, and we would get to see a drop in those numbers because of a drop in attempts.

At the time of writing, I know of only one airport terminal that has been built from an architectural design that is specifically oriented toward security. The 1986 opening of Terminal #4 at London's Heathrow Airport revealed this only example.

It is an imposing structure currently used for most British Airways flights and a handful of smaller airlines from sensitive areas of the world; El Al and South African Airways for example.

Working in concert with security experts, the architects attempted to blend the need for crowd control, direction, and containment with streamlined security "choke points" equipped with the most modern technology of search and detection. This all had to be accomplished with esthetically pleasing decor. Covert screening and surveillance ability has been built into the structure, and central control and isolation of specific areas can be accomplished by a small number of trained personnel because of the actual layout of the boarding gates. The completed job is very well done and will serve as a practical model to be tested and improved with experience.

An Ounce of Prevention

That experience may then be incorporated in the design of other terminals throughout the world. Even the most recent airports in the United States, such as Dallas-Forth Worth and Atlanta-Hatfield, encompassed the old concepts of maximum flow of passengers in and out with a minimum of delay and "choke points." This is doubly unfortunate because the needs of security demand that passenger flow be slowed and at times even stopped and that containment of areas and crowds of people should be in small "bite-size" pieces. For example, if a hostage problem can be isolated quickly and within a small physical area with the least number of hostages *or potential hostages,* you have what is called in military or law-enforcement parlance "a contained situation." That is a situation that has little or no chance of extending beyond the perimeter you have around it. The smaller the perimeter, the smaller the problem.

It is far easier to deal with a few hostages in a bank than a larger number in a supermarket, for example. Old design airport terminals invariably mean crowds of people in broad areas and easy access to multiple gates and aircraft. A newer terminal designed with security in mind breaks the crowds into smaller groups and isolates boarding areas and, therefore, aircraft from each other.

Anyone who has traveled in the past two years can testify to the chaotic bedlam typical of today's airline terminals. Piles of baggage scattered like obstacles through which you must wend your way as you dodge screaming kids, strollers, backpacks, and other traps for the unwary. Long lines at the check-in counters—even those for passengers with tickets who only wish to check their baggage. I really don't know whether it is just me, but I always, I mean *always,* get stuck behind someone who is either buying a ticket around the world involving eight different airlines or someone who is already ticketed and booked for a trip around the world and now wants to change the middle portion of it. As I prefer not to believe that God has singled me out, I assume you, too, know what I mean!

For good measure, one must add to the turmoil those many close families who feel a deep obligation to array themselves like a Greek chorus to bid farewell or hello to the one departing or arriving relative they have flocked to see. They too take up a considerable amount of space and add to the cacophony of noise that assails ones senses in the usually cavernous confines of the average airport terminal building. Mix in a healthy portion of nervousness and a dash of genuine fear, stir with an unceasing, intrusive, incomprehensible paging system, manned (or should I say womanned?) by nasal-toned mutilators of the English language, and you have an average American airport.

Now I invite you to take a look at this rich slice of humanity and attempt to see it all from the viewpoint of an airport security chief. He or she knows that to perform a 100 percent check of all passengers and baggage (carry-on and checked baggage), a minimum check-in time before flight will be three hours. That is from the moment you arrive until you are sitting in the airplane with the doors closed. Three hours! The bedlam just described occurs when passengers check in one hour before departure. There is not one major airport in the United States that could accommodate such a three-hour check-in requirement. What then can be done?

There are two basic considerations when ground-handling passengers outbound or transitting on flights. The first is the commercial need to get them processed through ticketing, baggage check-in, and seat assignment, and then, two, to move them physically onto the correct aircraft through the right gate.

Airport authorities make this process seem even more like running a gauntlet by impeding the path with all manner of "speciality shops" catering to what seems to be the most bizarre whims at outrageous prices. Okay—newspapers or something else to read on the flight is understandable, but who in heaven's name wants to purchase a $2 T-shirt for $12? I know of two major East Coast airports, one of them horrendously busy, which in the sterile area beyond the security checkpoint sells live lobsters, of all things. The flight attendants won't cook 'em for you in flight—does one buy them as pets? "Hi, honey, I'm glad to be home. See, I bought you a two-pound lobster to keep you company while I'm away on my business trips—only cost me $25." (It is an interesting sociological fact that many fads first show up in airport terminals—nut stands, dried fruit stands, tofu stands, croissant stands, etc.)

Anyway, the passenger is jostled, cajoled, herded, and generally bothered into going in the right direction until he or she reaches a choke point in the path. These are security checkpoints and control points where one of the two X-ray machines for checking hand baggage is invariably inoperative. It's like a scene from an old Western where the stampeding herd reaches a narrow pass. When the fellow in front of you sets off the alarm for the sixth time with his Marine Corps belt buckle or his four-pound ring of keys, it then becomes the scene where the herd runs into a blind canyon. You all mill around, muttering and looking at watches.

People who run airport terminals could do a much better job

of smoothing the passengers' way to the aircraft and at the same time improving security. It could be done by working within the existing physical layouts. Old designs may be adapted to modern threats. With careful planning, some order could be made out of the current chaos. Chicago's O'Hare Airport, New York's JFK and LaGuardia, Atlanta's Hatfield, Miami, Los Angeles, St. Louis's Lambert Field, Dallas-Fort Worth, all suffer in varying degrees from this easily fixable traffic problem. Indeed, having traveled through almost every airport terminal in the system, I cannot recall any which could not be improved by better planning and/or minor structural changes.

Many terminals of older design have interior wall structures that are easily removed. Moving a few walls around and creating new corridors leading to smaller, isolated gates or boarding areas would immediately have the effect of breaking up the mobs and focusing passengers to a particular gate or aircraft. Such passageways could be accomplished without introducing claustrophobia to already nervous passengers by using windows or walls made of the virtually unbreakable clear plastic available today. One may keep the appearance of space and the presence of light and yet break the potential problems down to "bite size" at the same time.

Redesign of the approach area at the front of terminals would also be an enormous boon to efficient movement of passengers. For example, a parking/drop-off area a short distance from the terminal with *preliminary* destination and flight identification accomplished for both passengers and baggage would be helpful. The passengers could then be whisked to the terminal on moving sidewalks or shuttle buses or trains. All non-passengers would be left behind. This would have the immediate effect of reducing the number of people inside the check-in area of the terminal, which is the first step toward improved security.

At one time there existed a number of downtown airline terminals in major cities throughout the world where one could check-in for a flight, check one's baggage and, for a small fee, be taken by bus to the airport for final processing and boarding. Is it time for both airlines and airport authorities to rethink the decision to close them down?

If downtown locations or existing airport space is at a premium, why not remote check-in terminals a few miles away and bus service from there? Anything that can be done to reduce the number of people and the resultant bedlam has to help, not only for security but the general attitude of passengers as well.

A VAPOR DETECTION or a thermal neutron explosive-detection device would be major turning points in the business of protecting passengers, crews, and aircraft from harm. Such a system could utilize a moving belt that would carry the checked bags from the check-in desk through the explosive-detection device. If the detector activated, then a computer-controlled robot arm would push the suspect bag off the conveyor belt and alert a security officer who could then examine the bag with care and in great detail.

The ultimate in such screening for explosives will be when technology permits us to place explosive-detection devices in the outflow valve of an aircraft.

To fly at great altitudes, aircraft have to be pressurized to provide a cabin atmosphere approximately like that to be found on the ground or at least high-altitude places on the ground. The atmosphere may range from the most dense at sea level (like New York) to the least dense at five thousand feet (like Denver). To accomplish this, compressed air is tapped from one or more of the jet engines at the compressor stage and pumped into the cabin, flight deck, and cargo compartments. When the pressure reaches the desired pressure, an outflow valve, usually located aft and in the belly of the fuselage, opens and relieves the pressure.

The controls may be set so that the entire body of air in the aircraft passes over the outflow valve while the aircraft is still at the gate, engines running and doors closed. When future technology permits, a probe in the outflow valve would detect the presence of explosives *somewhere* in the aircraft and electronically alert the aircraft's captain. He or she when so alerted would simply shut off the engines, and deplane everyone to allow a thorough search by means of a bomb-sniffing dog or thorough hand search.

How soon before such marvelous protections are available? In the early 1980s some research had been done on the development of an explosive-detection device, but interest and funds were low. In a perfect example of the tenet that it is an ill wind that doesn't blow anyone some good, the dramatic hijacking of TWA 847 in 1985 stirred an already concerned Congress into angry wakefulness. As a result, an initial $5 million expenditure for accelerated research and development in explosive-detection devices was included in the International Security and Development Cooperation Act of 1985. In addition, the Federal Aviation Administration projects expenditures of

An Ounce of Prevention

$11,800,000 in fiscal 1986 and an additional $12,700,000 in fiscal year 1987. Informed opinion indicates that by the end of that period working models suitable for *baggage* checking will become available. Explosive-detection devices to check people will come later as will the ultimate outflow-valve system we can still only dream of right now.

Meanwhile, we have the well known and currently available bomb-detectors and man's best friend—the dog. People constantly ask why more dogs are not trained and used to check all checked baggage. It's a fair question, but the answer is not encouraging. Admittedly, dogs are good at detecting explosives (incidentally gerbils are even better), but a dog's "nose" gets tire very quickly. They are generally used when a threat is known and are therefore engaged in a hunt for something specific or at least suspected. General scanning would soon tired the dog's "nose," or it would lose interest quickly. Additionally, dogs are very expensive to first train and then maintain, for each requires a human handler who is the dog's master and constant companion. Bomb-detector dogs do a superb job in the limited operational envelope they operate in but will never be able to do the job necessary to scan and clear that mountain of luggage and cargo carried by the airlines each day.

The price of security must be eternal vigilance and the judicious use of intelligence.

7

Defenses Against Terrorism In the Air

As mentioned earlier, the primary form of defense against attacks on civil aviation is pre-board screening, but there are further steps that can be taken right up to the point where you, the passenger, can play an important role in guarding civil aviation from terrorist attacks.

Let us start with the defenses that may begin as you approach the airport in preparation for a departure. At a number of airports considered to be high risk, your bus, taxi, or car may be stopped at a checkpoint set up some distance from the terminal. Anything from a cursory glance to a full identification process may occur here. While the number of airports where this takes place is few, it is considered to be a good first line of defense, *especially* when such checkpoints are set up on a seemingly random basis, or at least when periods of strict control are imposed on a random basis. Apart from the obvious security benefits derived from such checks, the random factor provides an element of surprise or of the unknown for a would-be terrorist, and such unknowns keep them off balance and fearful of what might happen next.

Assuming that you pass through such a checkpoint, if it exists, the next line of defense is drawn at the airline check-in counter. Here begins a series of covert and overt security checks that you will encounter on your way to your flight. One is the hijacker or terrorist "profile."

It is unfortunately now well known that such a profile exists. Once part of the covert array of defenses, the profile has become public knowledge, thanks to the inability of the news media to use good sense in its holy "pursuit of the truth." However, the one bright spot remaining in this instance is that the form and substance of the profile is not known. I have seen many articles published that claim to describe the elements, but in all cases the reports were incorrect. The profile itself is devilishly clever in its construction and remarkably easy to apply. Its elements are not obvious, and as it is being applied to you by a trained ticket airline check-in agent *or other airline or airport personnel,* you will be totally unaware of its application. Supplementing the profile are other covert surveillance techniques that help to confirm or verify the results of using the profile.

It is interesting to note that when the first profile was developed back in the early 1970s, basic as it was, when applied retroactively to previous known incidents, the profile fitted in well over 90 percent of them. This was and is remarkable when you understand that this early prototype profile was a simple, uncomplicated technique that could be learned in fifteen minutes by anyone with a grade-school eduation. With the experience gained since those early days and the change in the threat assessment, the profile has matured and has become increasingly sophisticated. Nevertheless, it is still simple and highly successful and undergoes constant review and refinements in response to experience and ongoing research.

We discussed earlier what happens to your baggage destined to go into the cargo hold of the aircraft. Various methods are used by the airlines to ensure that when a passenger checks a bag or bags for a flight, the passenger also gets on that flight. In other words, there must be an accompanying passenger for all checked baggage. If such a passenger fails to board, then all bags are unloaded and have to be physically identified by those passengers who were on board. Any unidentified bags are checked by security. There have been a number of acts of sabotage prevented by this simple but effective technique. Of course, this would not guard against a suicide terrorist mission, but such operations are a whole lot rarer than one would think. The reasons for this will be covered later when we examine the terrorist in detail.

NOW THAT YOU are checked in, you head toward the assigned boarding gate. The first notable security check comes at the X-ray machine and magnetometer or metal detector. This method of pre-board passenger screening is known as the sterile concourse concept.

Most airports have set up these security checkpoints at the entrance to departure gate fingers or concourses. This is the long (and when you are in a hurry and carrying a heavy bag, seemingly endless) structure that radiates out from the main central terminal and to which the aircraft nestle nose into, like piglets sucking at a sow. Indeed, when one recognizes that the nourishment an airliner must have to survive is passengers, the analogy is certainly a good one.

There are a few airports that do not employ the central hub-and-spoke architectural design. These have terminals that are built in the form of arcs where the distance from the outside roadway to the aircraft is only as deep as the terminal building itself. This, of course, is enormously convenient for passengers but, unfortunately, does not lend itself to a good, economical security setup for pre-board screening. At such airports, the airlines or airport authorities are obliged to provide such screening at each boarding gate, which is an enormous task both in terms of personnel and equipment.

Your carry-on items have passed through the X-ray machine under what we hope is the watchful eye of the operator, and you have passed through the magnetometer. Let us pause here for a moment and closely examine this highly visible and important line of defense.

The X-ray machines in use are mostly low-pulse X rays, which flash an image onto a television monitor screen a second or so after scanning an object. Continuous research goes on in the refinement of existing technology and the development of new machines that will provide higher resolution and clearer identification of a greater number of items and materials. There are a number of exciting developments coming in this field, and as the new generation of X-ray devices come on line, this particular line of defense will become harder and harder to penetrate.

There is, however, one vital element in this defense mechanism that cannot be engineered to improve performance. I refer, of course, to the operator. The human factor, which at the same time is the wonder of life and the bane of existence, plays the vital role in this marriage of man and machine. The machine may be, and indeed is, checked several times a day to ensure performance within established parameters. All it needs is a supply of electricity and some occasional maintenance, and it will work uncomplainingly and continuously day and night. Despite doing the same thing over and over again, it doesn't get bored or tired and consequently never needs motivation.

What then of its human partner? Who is that person and what is required of him or her? The people who operate these X-ray machines play a key role in the protection of billions of dollars worth of aircraft and millions of lives, and yet we know little of them.

Anyone who works for an honest living should have the deep respect of his or her fellow humans. From brain surgeon to janitor, nuclear physicist to field hand, each in his or her own way is contributing to society instead of living off it. Most people's rule of thumb would be the higher the responsibilities, education, and skills, the higher the compensation. Now that's only a rule of thumb of course, for one only has to listen to the inarticulate mumbling of multimillion-dollar-a-year sports and rock "stars" on television talk shows to realize that their communication skills can be reduced to the phrase "y'know." As to their contribution to human society, I best leave that to you, but I will say that in the order of things of importance, they contribute less than those who man the security checkpoints at airports.

Why then are those who man airport security checkpoints

almost exclusively drawn from the ranks of the lower end of the socioeconomic scale? Since the job pays at best only a little more than a minimum wage, the obvious answer is that airlines and others responsible for aviation security are anxious to do it at the lowest possible cost.

One frequently hears calls from members or committees of Congress and frequently from air travelers for an increase in the "quality" of people manning those security checkpoints. While I am sure that these calls and comments are not meant in a disparaging manner they, nevertheless, indicate that the aforementioned rule of thumb is being applied. Low skill level plus low educational level equals low pay plus poor performance—ergo, bad security.

What we must first understand here is that we are dealing with humans, not automobiles, though an analogy does exist. Undoubtedly a Jaguar outperforms a Ford Escort, but what use is all that power of the sleek, expensive Jaguar if the car is being driven exclusively in rush-hour city traffic? I can tell you from experience that weekly tune-ups would be necessary if one were driven in such conditions while, on the other hand, your average Ford Escort will hum happily forever in a like situation. Briefly stated, while both cars are intended to provide personal transportation, they are equipped to meet specific operational needs and presumably economic needs also.

Those worthy people who operate and monitor the security machines meet the specific operational and economic needs of the task. If one were to select and pay operators from the higher levels of skill, education, and economic scale, then one would have a Jaguar that would be unable to cope with the task.

Looking at a television screen displaying black and white

images of the contents of people's hand luggage is not exactly stimulating and interesting work. Bluntly, it is boring and repetitious. Put a Ph.D. in front of that screen, and he or she wouldn't make it through one shift. His mind and attention would be constantly distracted by outside and intellectual stimuli, and you could slip a bazooka past him. Those that operate the machines are also intellectual but, because of the usual lower level of society as we measure it in terms of education, are less easily distracted from the job at hand.

This is not to say, however, that they can sit there for a full shift of several hours and maintain good vigilance for concealed weaponry. Indeed, such assumptions have led to breaches of security in the past. Not enough study has been performed on how long a person can effectively perform such tasks and, further, how one may provide incentives to maintain a high level of performance. Right now many authorities are employing the stick-and-carrot method. Operators who fail to recognize weapons introduced into the system, either by terrorists or authorities who covertly check the system by attempting to penetrate it, are disciplined in some manner. The operator who fails to spot a test weapon is immediately identified by the inspector introducing the weapon into the system. In cases where hostile weapons have gotten through, it has sometimes been possible to identify the checkpoint and time of security penetration by backtracking events with the help of eye witnesses who remember seeing the hijacker or terrorist.

Those that catch the weapons get some reward. This works to a certain degree, but more has to be done. Studies and tests of optimum stretches of duty and commensurate breaks, rotation of duties from checking the television screen to loading the bags into the machine or operating the magnetometer—in other words, cross training to provide variety—these are things that need study by industrial science.

One of the greatest motivators for anyone is a feeling of self-esteem and importance. The rent-a-cop companies that provide most of the checkpoint personnel tacitly recognize this insofar as they provide their personnel with a halfway decent uniform of quasi-military or law-enforcement design. The positive effects of this are offset, however, by the inevitable feeling of impermanence and lack of career potential in low-paid jobs.

This is an area where unions can help. Membership in a good labor union gives one a feeling of belonging. It provides one with a certain sense of security against arbitrary discipline or dismissal and ultimately could provide that most important human right: a living wage as opposed to a minimum wage. Such improvements will come about only if these workers get themselves organized. If they do, then conditions will change to the point that you, the air-traveling public, will reap the benefits by way of the increased level of security that will ensue.

The magnetometer or related detector is used in conjunction with the X-ray checks for the presence of a mass of metal sufficient to set off the alarm on your person. The metal does not have to be in one piece; it could, like a handgun, be broken down to component parts and distributed to various parts of your body. The magnetometer will, however, detect the aggregate amount of metal and squeal on you.

I am frequently asked by friends and acquaintances why they can pass through one checkpoint with this belt buckle or bunch of keys but trigger the alarm at others? The machines

Defenses Against Terrorism in the Air

have variable settings on them with federally prescribed limits of sensitivity within which they must be operated. One set at the lower limit may not find your bunch of keys while another set at the upper limit will. Add to this the occasional operator who in response to a tiresome number of false alarms will break the rules and lower the sensitivity to a level below that required by regulation. Most of the time, however, indeed in the vast majority of cases, this particular form of checking will reveal the presence of a small handgun or other dangerous weapon.

CONTINUING ON YOUR way to the boarding gate, you will then undergo another form of profiling at the gate area either as you check at the gate desk and/or as you show your boarding pass to the agent just before you step into the jetway or out onto the ramp. On certain flights considered to be high risk or vulnerable, your hand baggage may go through a thorough hand search and you may have a body pat-down or check over with hand-held, portable metal detectors.

If such ancillary checking is in place at the point of boarding, you will undoubtedly be given an additional profile to supplement the others you previously unknowingly experienced. It will consist of the same covert basic elements and questions with a couple of added features designed to further check you. For obvious reasons, details of such methods must remain secret. Most, if not all of the time, you will be unaware of this profiling, or, indeed, any of the covert screening that you have passed through from the time you entered the front door of the terminal until you board the aircraft.

Like store detectives on the lookout for shoplifters, undercover security personnel are mingling undetectably among the throngs of people at all points of the pre-check-in, check-in, and boarding process. They are trained to spot the unusual and the suspicious and just like a cop develops street sense and can pick out a bad one as he or she cruises a busy street, so can these undercover guards "sense" a wrong one on their "beat" too.

NOW YOU ARE on board and comfortably seated; you doubtlessly think that you have passed through the last mesh in the ever-diminishing size nets on the way to the plane. Well, that is not entirely true, for while you may have completed the obstacle course of *pre-board screening,* you are still being scrutinized by the flight attendants on board the aircraft.

Properly trained and motivated crew members, pilots and flight attendants, make first-rate security *checkers.* There are few people who spend more time in and around aircraft and airport environments than flight crew members. Airplanes and airports are their workplace, and they are as familiar with them as a shopkeeper with his store, a businesswoman with her office, or a machinist with his factory. Anything out of place jumps to their attention.

I am frequently asked, as a pilot, how I can constantly monitor the bewildering array of instruments that bedeck the inside of an airliner cockpit. A pilot develops a scan pattern whereby every few seconds his or her eyes sweep the whole instrument panel. This becomes as natural as breathing in and out and is just as automatic. The sweep probably takes only a second or a second and a half, so you may wonder how anyone can ready fifty gauges in such a brief moment. Well, of course, one cannot. What the pilot is trained to see is not the readings on the gauges but *indications of something out of place*. If you walk into your living room you don't have to note the position of every piece of furniture to detect immediately that a familiar picture is missing from a wall or a lamp has been repositioned. In other words, you already know what the scene is supposed to look like, and you notice only if something has changed.

The same applies to crew members. Anything out of place in their environment will attract their attention. It is important, however, that they be trained to recognize when they see something out of place, for people have a natural tendency to see what they expect to see. This is why for centuries magicians or, more properly, illusionists have been amazing people with their tricks. To illustrate my point of looking but not seeing, you can try the following experiment with a friend. If you notice that he is wearing an analog-type watch, cover up the watch with your hand and ask him how long he has owned the watch. Let's assume that five years is the answer. Then get him to agree that he probably looks at his watch at least ten times a day. By now you have established that he has looked at an item about the size of a postage stamp more than 17,000 times. Now ask him what denotes the six o'clock position on the watchface. It is a Roman or Arabic numeral, a dash, a dot, a day/date window without any designation?

You can bet money that better than 90 percent will not know or be able to guess correctly. After your friend has answered or guessed, uncover the watch and let him look. Once he has looked, cover the watch again, then point out that he has just looked at his watch and ask him what the *exact* time is! Ten to one odds he will not know. People see but they do not observe.

That little experiment was used on me many years ago when I was being trained as a fighter-reconnaissance pilot. That particular job entailed flying over enemy territory at very high speed and extreme low altitude to avoid detection and antiaircraft fire. One maybe got one second over the target area to take photographs and memorize the scene, i.e., the position of tanks or heavy artillery, how many bivouacs, and so forth. At debriefing one was expected to describe these to an intelligence officer for analysis.

Criminologists frequently employ the use of hypnotism as a means of getting details of what a witness subconsciously *observed* beyond what his conscious *saw*.

So it all comes down to training and more training to keep a sharp edge on one's wits. The industry has recognized this finally and is beginning to tap the enormous resource of aircrew members for enhancing the security system. Crew members are also particularly useful in noting breaches of the system and can quickly report them and have them corrected; so they act as a checking agent, too.

So now we have established that the nice woman or man who serves you coffee or gets you a pillow is a properly trained security observer. This, I would point out, is in addition to the other primary duty of being on board that aircraft to take care of you in case of an emergency. The coffee-and-pillow routine is an extra provided by the airline and is entirely ancillary to a flight attendant's primary function and purpose.

Can we then expect them to be ready to kung-fu a terrorist in the aisle? Unlikely, for I hope that the only time you will ever see a flight attendant inflict violence on anyone is if she is female and gets her behind pinched by an obstreperous passenger!

Defenses Against Terrorism in the Air

Well, you may ask, if the flight attendants are not going to protect me and save me from a terrorist on board, I guess it must therefore be up to the pilots up there in the sharp end of this aluminum tube. I hate to shatter anyone's heroic illusions, especially those one may hold about airline pilots, but those guys up front are most unlikely to become involved in any physical activity with terrorists on board.

There are a number of very good practical reasons for this reluctance on behalf of pilots and flight attendants, and none has anything to do with personal bravery or lack of it.

One of the most common ploys used by terrorists on any mission that takes place in a "contained" area such as an aircraft, train, or ship is to have "sleepers" concealed within the hostage group. One or more of the terrorists will act as hostages throughout an entire operation and, even after an escape has been made, frequently continue to conceal their true identity or role. They are there in the event that the primary terrorists are taken out by some means. If that happens then they, the sleepers, are in a position to retake the aircraft, train, or ship and salvage the mission. They also provide a spy within the hostages to uncover any plots that may be developing against their kidnappers. Another good reason for sleepers is that they provide supervision as well as backup for the primary terrorists who frequently are from the lower echelons of their particular organization. I will discuss this aspect in greater detail when we examine the terrorists themselves.

In many of the hijackings organized by Middle-East paramilitary terrorists, the presence of sleepers has been almost certain. Because they tend to reveal themselves only *if absolutely necessary,* it is difficult to confirm such suspicions. It is known that in the early hijackings of the TWA, BOAC, and Swissair flights to the Jordan Desert by Leila Khaled and her associates, passengers formerly believed to be innocent victims by the other hostages, were greeted warmly by their captors upon deplaning, thereby revealing their true role.

In addition to the sleeper problem, crew members are discouraged from attacking terrorists. Crew members are not armed; most pilots are often familiar with weapons from military training, but such familiarity is frequently rusty. Even in the hands of an expert, a handgun is not a weapon that will guarantee a kill. I have known of many people who have been shot several times and still continued to function and represent a threat. Shoot a terrorist and he or she might pull a grenade on you, and you've got a heap of trouble on your hands.

If crews were armed it wouldn't take much imagination for a terrorist to take a flight attendant or passenger hostage and threaten his life to get a substantial increase in his arsenal. As we have seen, pilots do not want *any* guns on board their aircraft—"good" guns have a habit of becoming "bad" guns by the simple expedient of changing hands.

Finally, it has been proven over and over that the best way of protecting lives is to *contain* a situation. This means that all who play some defensive role in the situation, such as aircrews and outside law enforcement or security forces, try not to let the situation escalate in scope or violence and that the "world" of the incident is confined to the aircraft, ship, building, or whatever the structure being seized is. By containing it one introduces a constant, almost a routine, which can turn a bizarre situation into one with a semblance of normalcy. Curiously, a rapport or bonding inexorably begins to develop between captor and captives with a commensurate attitude that those "outside" represent the threat. This physiological phenomena affects both hostages and hostage-takers. It is so well defined that it even has its own name in the lexicon of psychiatry; the Stockholm Syndrome. The name was derived from a situation that occurred in Stockholm, Sweden, in the 1960s when a gang of bank robbers got trapped in a bank vault with some hostages for several days. At the end of the ordeal, the hostages were released unharmed but with a curious empathy and comradeship with the bank robbers. Indeed, romance had sprung forth between one victim and her captor.

The Stockholm Syndrome is a good, protective happening inasmuch as the terrorists' anger and actions tend to be directed to those *outside* the contained situation, which, of course, has the effect of diminishing the threat to the hostages. Crews are trained to recognize this may happen to the passengers and, indeed, are told that they, too, will to varying degrees be irresistibly caught up in the syndrome.

In the final analysis, death or injury to a crew member, whether pilot or flight attendant, will seriously affect the overall safety of the flight, for each has an important and sometimes vital role to play in the operation of the flight. In brief, a risk/reward analysis would clearly indicate that crew member heroics are not in the best interests of the flight, passengers, and situation in general.

UP UNTIL THE dramatic and tragic hijacking of TWA 847 in June 1985, flight crew security training was largely a hit-or-miss matter. Airlines struggling to lower costs in the cutthroat competitiveness of a deregulated industry had little time or inclination to spend money on items not directly related to improving the bottom line. Efforts by the Air Line Pilots Association and even the Office of Civil Aviation Security of the Federal Aviation Administration to significantly improve and increase security training for flight and ground crews were vigorously resisted by the airlines and their trade association, the Air Transport Association (ATA).

TWA flight 847 changed that. The event was dramatic and politically sexy. Representatives from both houses of Congress were falling over each other introducing aviation security bills and holding hearings. The public was in an uproar.

Seeing a window of opportunity open, the Air Line Pilots Association leaped through it with proposals to Congress to upgrade security, increase crew training, and fund research and development of explosive-detection devices. As we have seen, TWA flight 847 was a classic example of an ill wind blowing somebody some good.

As a result of resultant legislation, these things came to pass and now, when you fly on an airline of the United States, your cockpit and cabin crew are the best trained security crew members in the world (with the possible exception of El Al).

IN ADDITION TO the training in the physiological containment of a situation and the previously mentioned awareness and observation techniques, other training covers such matters as explosive recognition and handling of explosive devices in flight.

This aspect is particularly a specialist matter, for explosive devices come in a variety of forms and guises. A book, a briefcase, a child's lunchbox all can be bombs, and, if they have no identifiable owner, they should be treated as though they are. When we get to the part where I describe the role that you can play in the security net, I will point out what you, the passenger, can do about this particularly deadly threat. The crew member knows what to do, for he or she has now been trained and will for the rest of an active career go through recurrent training at least once a year and even more frequently when new techniques and methods are developed.

SO NOW WE have taken care of all those folks who take care of you inside the aircraft, but what about the outside. While you are still at the boarding gate and sitting by a window, take a look outside at what is going on. There are trucks, tugs, carts, strange vehicles you can't put a name to, people in overalls, people in uniform, people in street clothes, all milling around with an air of purpose, but, you may ask, what the devil are they all doing?

To prepare a flight for departure you have mechanics, baggage loaders, commissary or caterers, fuelers, cleaners, lavatory tank trucks and operatives (colloquially known as "honey wagons"); there are people ensuring the safe loading of United States mail and, on occasion, menacing-looking people supervising the safe loading of bullion or other valuable cargo.

Scattered throughout this crowd of aircraft attendants are trained ground security personnel. They are looking for anything out of the ordinary and are checking for the photo IDs that everyone with access to the air-side or operational side of an airport must display on their outermost garments in clear view.

Supplementing these security people are the workers themselves or at least those in the employ of the airline. As part of their training and recurrent training, they are required to have a level of security knowledge and skill just like pilots and flight attendants. These requirements are different, for their piece of the aviation scene is different; but, nevertheless, their participation and observation are essential elements in the vast security net that is draped across your flight and, indeed, the whole of civil aviation in the United States. These people, while providing additional layers of security, have the potential for also creating harm.

In the United States, CBS's "60 Minutes" and others from the print and audio news media have taken great delight in discovering and revealing how easy it is to get a job as a cleaner or other airport worker with the flimsiest—in some cases, phony—identification. This cavalier attitude of airline and airport personnel directors toward background checks of people who will have access to the operational side of airports is astonishing to say the least. Their failure in this area is irresponsible and reprehensible.

The attendant publicity following such revelation by "60 Minutes" and others has done much to tighten federal regulations concerning in-depth background checks of airport personnel. The net result of these revelations has been a great improvement in the checking and hiring practices of airlines and airport authorities.

TO REPEAT SOMETHING I said earlier to dissuade you of the idea that those of us engaged in the airline business now skulk around eyeing everyone suspiciously, we are trained to notice things *out of the ordinary*. As a result of this enhanced training

Defenses Against Terrorism in the Air

the safety and security of your flight has been increased immeasurably.

IN ADDITION TO this industry force, there are, of course, a number of outside government agencies involved in protecting you as a passenger from terrorist attacks.

The most obvious and visible one is the Office of Civil Aviation Security of the Federal Aviation Administration. In the more than sixteen years of dealing with them, I have never come across a more dedicated and, pound for pound, more effective group of federal employees than the men and women of this department. With responsibility for everything from profiles to bombs, they have managed as a small, underfunded group to pack ten pounds of need into a five-pound bag.

When a hijacking or other terrorist attack against civil aviation takes place, a variety of departments of government swing into action. Within the F.A.A. Command Center in Washington is a communications system that can reach anywhere in the world. From an explosives specialist on a golf course to a pilot in flight over an ocean on the other side of the world, they can patch through a direct voice communication and provide expert assistance when and where it is needed.

The Federal Bureau of Investigation has had an active, indeed a key role in protecting civil aviation. Apart from the obvious criminal detection and apprehension functions performed by the FBI, they have what are unquestionably the best, most effective teams of hostage negotiators in the world. Their developed skills in this surprisingly effective technique have passed from being a science to an art, and the FBI hostage training course is the benchmark for everyone else.

TERROR IN THE SKIES

There is nothing magical about good hostage negotiations. It's fair to say that the embryo for this training had its roots in special departments within major U.S. city police forces, mainly the New York City Police Department. Because of the number of suicides or would-be suicides who frequently chose one of the many high places available in New York City as their intended last stand on earth, certain police officers became known for their instinctive ability to talk or negotiate with a "jumper" and talk them out of it. At the very least, such early, crude negotiations had the effect of containing the situation until suitable rescue equipment and personnel arrived. A Sergeant Frank Boltz of the New York City Police Department made quite a name for himself in this regard and frequently had to turn his developing skills from unhappy suicides to dangerous hostage-takers. It was then discovered that the techniques used worked equally well in either situation.

Study and refinement of Frank Boltz's techniques were undertaken by the FBI, and by the middle of the 1970s the bureau had the basis for a training course. The success of the FBI is extraordinary, and their batting average is well into the 900s. Special Agents are carefully selected for the right personality, voice, and manner. They must have enormous patience, a strong will, and a capacity for understanding aberrant behavior. They undergo intensive training in psychology. Political science and current events round off the world-renowned school they operate at the FBI Academy in Quantico, Virginia.

I have personally watched on three occasions seemingly impossible situations of gross threat end with surrender by the hostage-takers. To reveal the techniques would be a violation of law and trust, but I will say this: I will never, ever play poker with an FBI hostage negotiator!

Defenses Against Terrorism in the Air

When the incident under management is international, the Department of State becomes involved and, in fact, within the Department of State exists an Office for Combatting Terrorism under the leadership of a full ambassador and staff. At one time that job was considered to be a "holding pattern" for career diplomats awaiting assignments to a more traditional post, but with the escalation of threat level, it has become a job of some prestige with a commensurate increase in responsibility and worry-factor.

The Central Intelligence Agency and other intelligence arms of the United States also play a vital role in crisis management insofar as they provide intelligence on the terrorists involved and the faction they come from. Contacts and communications for the purposes of "doing a deal" can often be affected by the covert agencies of our government. For reasons that should be obvious, I will not elaborate any further on these activities.

Last, but certainly not least, comes the Department of Defense. The various branches of the military offer a variety of services: communications, transportation, weaponry, intelligence, and most publicized of all, the "Delta Force." Yes, indeed, there is a Delta Force, though until revealed by our ever-faithful news media, even the name was classified. The Delta Force is one of a number of inter-service, specialized military personnel who have excruciatingly specialized training in the rescue of hostages and the taking of highly sensitive targets. Their counterparts abroad are the Special Air Service (SAS) of Great Britain, the Group Nine Force of West Germany, and the Specialist force of Israel.

If one can get by the glamour and hyperbole of Hollywood and news reporters, you would find men capable of performing extraordinary tasks under impossible conditions. Again, this is an area that is so sensitive that further revelation would at best be harmful and at worst totally irresponsible; so you will have to rely upon your own assessment in deciding how much of the publicity is real. Suffice it to say that the existence of such a capacity in our arsenal against terrorism is considered by everyone else involved to be a major blessing.

In conclusion, you can see the enormous number of organizations and people involved in the protection of *your* flight, and if the ultimate tragedy occurs and you do become a hostage at least you have the comfort of knowing that this prodigious amount of knowledge, skills, manpower, and resources, in all its awesome array, is in action, employed to ensure your survival. You will never be alone.

8

The Terrorists and You

Having seen all that others do to ensure your protection and safety, what can you do to protect yourself?

Before answering that question, one must determine what degree of concern exists, for it can range from sensible concern to hysteria.

Many articles and publications, cashing in on the upper range of the panic scale, have taken to producing extensive lists of do's and don'ts for air travelers and others. To comply with their suggestions, you would need an entire course in survival and a "how to go undercover and stay there" training regime worthy of the CIA or the National Security Agency. In fact, many of the recommendations have been lifted from such training courses and manuals.

TERROR IN THE SKIES

If you feel that such excessive protective attitudes are for you, then I can only suggest that if you are planning to travel for pleasure—don't! If you are traveling for business reasons (other than if you are an intelligence field operative)—get into a business that doesn't require you to travel.

Travel, as with most activities in life, is undertaken for either business or pleasure. Anytime you engage in any activity you encounter some risk. How much risk really depends upon how you wish to live your life.

Baseball history records the achievements of a first baseman named Zeke Bonura of the old Washington Senators. He was remarkable for his great size and astonishing immobility. He was famous for the several fielding awards he collected during his career, all of which extolled his remarkable lack of fielding errors. Zeke had, early in his career, stumbled upon the basic truth of baseball defense—the fewer the number of times you handle the ball the fewer errors you can be charged with.

Now you can apply the Zeke Bonura theory to your life and avoid travel at all costs, but then again, what risk does that put you at?

For example, probably the most hardheaded business people are executives of insurance companies. In comparison, bankers are jolly philanthropists. Most insurance company rates are based on perceived risk calculated from statistical analysis and historical trends. Actuarial tables have their genesis in such statistics and trends.

If one were to examine the ascribed risk factors to what one would normally encounter in life, the insurance company would tell you that you are at greatest risk in or around your home. Most automobile accidents occur within ten miles of the home. Every year the death rates from accidental gunshots, burnings, electrocutions, falls, poisonings, crushings, and an entire gruesome catalogue of blood and carnage occur in the *safety* of the home.

Now, with the exception of a few mentally deranged folk, we all accept that we are mostly safe and secure within the confines of our particular abodes, be it a mansion or a one-room efficiency. The reason for this statistically wholly unwarranted attitude is that a home constitutes familiar surroundings and familiar surroundings do not suggest danger. Oh sure, most of us take some precautions. We install smoke detectors, locks on outside doors, and maybe even locks on windows. Some people even spring a few bucks to buy a fire extinguisher, if only for the kitchen, but by and large that's as far as we go.

If you recognize yourself in that group take comfort in being one of a majority. You could, of course, hire a company to "burglarproof" and "fire-protect" your home. You could have experts identify and correct every hazard, both existent and potential. If you can't afford that, you can buy books on the subject and do-it-yourself (though watch out for those power tools, they can be more dangerous than handguns). All in all you can give yourself a heart attack worrying about what could happen to you in your home. Most of us don't and continue to take what we deem to be reasonable, prudent actions to avoid domestic catastrophe.

When you travel you are actually statistically improving your chances of avoiding death and injury by leaving that place of poisoning, electrocution, falls, and so on. Of course, none of us view it that way and, indeed, we often take the opposite view. This is because we are traveling into the unknown or at least the unfamiliar. If familiarity breeds contempt, then surely unfamiliarity breeds fear. This shouldn't be particularly surprising or alarming, for it is a necessary and helpful defense mechanism that can help you *if not practiced to excess.*

With very few exceptions there are few dangers in life that cannot be avoided or at least ameliorated by a dose of plain common sense.

Humor has it that one should never play poker with a man called "Doc," dine at a place called "Mom's," or eat yellow snow! Experience and instinct make for good protection. Who among us would venture down a strange, dark alley or blow our car horn to get a pack of Hell's Angels to move out of our way? Precious few, but on the other hand millions of us still smoke despite the medical evidence, thousands experiment with "recreational" drugs, or drive at excessive speed, but most of these foolish acts or excesses are the result of one's own actions. The other stuff is much more frightening because the unpleasantness that could happen to you occurs from events outside of your initiative and control.

That statement in itself is basically true unless one examines closely a life-threatening situation created by a terrorist takeover of your flight. Have you lost all initiative and control?

One may reasonably argue that one's options of free expression are somewhat muted under the guns of trigger-happy political/religious fanatics. What one has to bear in mind, however, is that terrorists are vulnerable, too, for despite their fanaticism, they are having to cope with as many or more problems as you are faced with at that time.

LET US TAKE a look at what might be described as the classic hijacking/terrorist situation.

The Terrorists and You

Generally speaking, terrorists avoid hijacking Boeing 747s. The upper-deck remoteness of the flight deck and the sheer size of the aircraft and number of passengers makes it extremely difficult to control. Even the smaller wide-body aircraft such as the Douglas DC-10, Lockheed L-1011, or Airbus A-300 are less desirable due to their large size and commensurate passenger loads.

The smaller Boeing 727 or Douglas DC-9 or MD80s are far more attractive insofar as one can see from one end of the cabin to the other. The flight deck is easily accessible once the cockpit door has been unlocked, and the approximately 100 to 130 passengers they hold is a manageable crowd within the narrow confines of these aircraft.

Probably your attackers will number two (with, remember, the possibility of sleepers). Their command post will be set up in the first-class cabin because of its location and control over the cockpit and main exit door. It also has more moving around space and commands a view and field of fire rearward into the tourist section. It is reasonable to expect any resistance, gunfire, or whatever, to come from the rear compartment, and the presence of the pilots up front provides a deterrent to such foolhardy actions for, after all, who wants to risk disabling those who are flying the aircraft?

If there is more than one terrorist, the other or others will patrol throughout the entire aircraft. They will demand that you sit in your seats with your seat belts fastened and your hands on your heads. This latter instruction is later relaxed after they have searched everyone and everyplace for weapons.

There have been a number of hijackings where the terrorists

sought to identify and segregate Jewish passengers. If you are a Jew, you may wish to consider this and avoid carrying or wearing any artifacts or jewelry that would identify your religion. I have many Jewish friends who have developed a subconscious, self-protective life-style and manner although they themselves have never been in any life-threatening situation. Two thousand years of religious persecution must, I assume, create at least a subconscious survival instinct more finely honed than average. Such precautions as I have described would be prudent, and Christians may well bear in mind that Moslems do not care for them either, so their crucifixes and Saint Christopher medals may be drawing unwarranted attention to them. Having these things with you is really a personal decision you must make.

Indeed, if you have an obviously Jewish name, what are you going to do? Change it? One's name is one of the most precious possessions one can have. Why should fear cause you to permanently deny it?

Many hijackers have been common thieves as well, robbing their hostages of money, jewels, and other valuables. For reasons other than terrorism, you would be well advised to travel with little jewelry and carry only small amounts of cash (use travelers checks).

Anything else, such as cameras and other valuable, necessary accoutrements to your trip should be registered and insured. As I say, such precautions are sensible any time you travel. Again, a piece of advice that holds good for any travel situation is to take sufficient supplies of any medication with you, not in your checked baggage.

If you are involved in any sensitive intelligence, defense, or related job or industry, it would be prudent not to have any evidence of such involvement with you in the cabin.

In summary, keep a low profile to avoid attracting any special attention to yourself. If you go beyond this, it would appear that you have gone beyond reasonable concern and, perhaps, you should reevaluate your need to fly.

NOW LET'S TAKE an in-depth look at the terrorist.

Terrorists come in all sizes, colors, genders, motivations, ages, religions, and ethnic origins.

Those who operate from and in Europe are frequently well educated and come from good families. Some have come from backgrounds that could be considered to be privileged. The Baader Meinhof group and the Red Brigade, for example, consist of small numbers of young intellectuals. The bands are generally very small, usually less than twenty in number, and are given to indulging in kidnappings, assassinations of public figures, and random bombings. They tend to oppose the United States, the military buildup in Europe, capitalism, and any nation of conservative bent. They support nuclear disarmament, ecology, and communism, or at least some romanticized version of it.

They are especially dangerous because of the generally high level of intelligence, intellect, and education many of them display. Because of their small numbers and underground existence, they are difficult to detect and capture, and their similar radical backgrounds make them difficult to penetrate for the purpose of gathering information about their activities.

Something of a metamorphosis has taken place in their modus operandi since their formative years in the 1970s. There seems to be less and less desire for publicity, and, indeed, it seems almost as if their utter contempt for the public has left them only the satisfaction of performing the terrorist acts themselves. This curious turn is most worrisome because it is very difficult to deal or negotiate with people who wish to bring about change by terror alone and have no desire to extort change from the authorities. This is just a step away from nihilism. Fortunately they are few in numbers and their activities have been mostly confined to European and U.S. military targets in Europe.

While there is evidence of some peripheral involvement with attacks on civil aviation, they tend to leave the airlines alone. This is consistent with the seeming lack of interest in worldwide publicity. I would also like to think that intellectually they have realized that the airline system is now very well protected and offers great risk of detection and capture. Car bombs in areas where U.S. military personnel and their dependents shop are much safer targets as far as they are concerned.

Despite the seeming isolation of their bands, they are actively involved in the international terrorist network and can be relied upon for aid and comfort by terrorists from other parts of the world, especially the Middle East and Northern Ireland.

Turning to that unhappy land, Northern Ireland, we have the Provisional Irish Republican Army in the ranks of international terrorism. The enemy they fight is ostensibly exclusively British (although they manage to kill many of their fellow Irishmen as well) and, unlike the rest of the terror network, they are not anti-American. As for religious fervor,

The Terrorists and You

Catholicism is only a nominal requirement, and they do not attack Protestantism but only those who happen to be Protestants. In brief, within Northern Ireland the terror is purely secular with religion only a convenient form of identification. When engaged in terrorist attacks against British targets in England and other overseas places, even that distinction is lost, for they would just as soon kill English Catholics as English Protestants, Jews, or members of any other creed.

They tend also to operate in small bands, frequently unaware of each other's activity. They do avail themselves of the terrorist-training facilities in Libya, Iran, and Syria and, like their contemporaries in Europe, will give assistance to other terrorists within the international network.

On a personal level they fall largely into three categories: 1) the Romantic Intellectual, 2) the Criminal, and 3) the Bumpkin.

The Romantic Intellectual is the planner and thinker when it comes to operations that could be considered political. The assassination of a government official, the blowing up of a police station, the assassination of Lord Mountbatten: all such economically worthless endeavors are planned, executed, and occasionally carried out by this creature. Frequently well educated, he or she, but mostly he, burns with a fervor to reunite Ireland and will risk a great deal to play a historic and heroic role in its reunification. He is the stuff of which legends are made. He is Brian Collins, Kevin Barry, and the like from the early, first days of "The Troubles."

I became well acquainted with these legends as a small boy at my mother's knee. My mother, formerly Charlotte O'Gorman from Dublin, Eire, had grown up with her considerable family, some seven sisters and four brothers, during the time of "The Troubles." She claimed to have been present when the hated British "Black and Tans" troops, in reprisal for a terrorist attack by the IRA, drove onto the playing field in the middle of a hurling match (a peculiar Irish blood sport similar to lacrosse or field hockey) being played at the great Phoenix Park Sports Arena in Dublin and opened fire on the crowd with automatic weapons.

As a small lad it seemed that every male relative I had was involved in the war against the British. This produced a considerable confusion in me, for my father was English and presumably was a legitimate target for my mother's relatives!

I mention this to illustrate that even today I have difficulty in distinguishing between the fact and fiction surrounding the Irish cause. The romantics, and often those with intellect to match, have less trouble than I obviously had, and instead embrace the tales with the fervor of patriotism and a determination to do something about it.

Sincere and dedicated, they give the veneer of respectability to a gruesome campaign of death, maimings, and mayhem. They are the ones paraded before gatherings of misty-eyed Irish-Americans throughout the United States. They are the ones sent to march in the St. Patrick's Day parade in New York City, and they raise millions of dollars to buy the weapons of terror.

They are used by their own with the uncaring cynicism an Indian beggar will use to maim a child to elicit sympathetic contributions.

The Criminals are those who use the Romantic Intellectuals. These are the type whose antisocial propensities draw them to criminal activities, or better yet, the ability to perform criminal acts under the guise of revolution or fighting for freedom against repression. Bank robberies, holdups, muggings, drug dealing, even prostitution, are used ostensibly to gather money for the cause, although most of it sticks to the fingers of the field lieutenants. There is some irony in that these people of such antisocial and antisociety convictions should be protected and admired by large segments of respectable society. It has been demonstrated that many of them are criminal psychopaths and delight in the killing and maiming they engage in. One must ask, who else could kill a child in its crib for any reason, let alone an accident of birth that brought it into a Protestant family?

Certainly not the Bumpkin. He is the soldier, the gofer, the one who does the grunt work, drives the getaway car, delivers the weapons, transports the explosives. He is usually uneducated and bored and depressed by the grinding poverty and bleakness of country life or the squalor of decaying cities. The IRA offers a chance of excitement, money in the pocket, and, perhaps most important of all, a chance to belong to something and maybe be somebody.

Taken all together they constitute a pretty sorry gang of misfits, but, indeed, they do pose a dangerous threat to their enemies. Fortunately for the rest of the world, but unfortunately for the English, they do have a very narrow target.

Only because of their involvement in the international networking system of terrorism are they worthy of mention in the context of international terrorism.

OTHERS WHO FALL into this category are scattered throughout the world in small pockets, like festering sores on a body, but pale into insignificance next to the major cancer of Middle-East terrorists.

Here we are talking of the big leaguers, the heavy hitters, the group that immediately springs to mind when the phrase "international terrorist" is used. They are Carlos, the Jackal, Abu Nidal: figures of both fact and fiction and carefully contrived to blur the distinction between the two.

To most of us, these are the terrorists who are the most fascinating and frightening and yet, in reality we know little of them. Who are they and what are they and what can you do if they take you as a hostage?

9

Arab James Bonds or Psychopathic Killers?

Earlier we had talked of terrorism being created by the havenots and the dispossessed. We also recognized that terrorism can spring from forcing one's dogma upon another. We were, in essence, talking of terrorism in the Middle East.

To understand the whole picture, let us briefly examine some of the modern history of the Middle East and how the map came to look as it does today.

At the end of the Great War, or as it later became known, World War I, Arabia as it was then called was released from the crushing rule of the Turkish Ottoman Empire. The Allied governments, taking Arabia as part of the spoils of war, divided up the entire massive area into a number of artificially created nations; Jordan, Palestine, Syria, Iraq, and so forth.

Each was placed under the internal control of a king or

prince carefully selected and sometimes created by the conquering European nations. As the general attitude prevailed that there was nothing of intrinsic value to be had from such a place other than the sea of oil on which it floated, its only other value was strategic because of the "choke points" (a modern term) it geographically commanded, thereby providing impressive control over major shipping lanes.

In general the population was treated by Europeans and other non-Arabs with the same disdain shown by their previous master, the Turks, though it must be said with much less cruelty. This was at a time in the history of the world when the sun never did set on the British Empire and that odd mixture of fair play and discrimination so unique to the British was standard in the colonized territories and countries. The individual Arab was, at best, patronized and at worst treated with contempt, and so it remained up to the advent of World War II. Then the nations that comprised Arabia became suddenly and dramatically essential for their oil and strategic locations.

Political courtship of the ruling families in the Arab and Gulf State nations was a major undertaking of the Allied and Axis nations. Sensing a propitious and probably never-to-be-repeated opportunity, those being wooed extracted great promises from their suitors and sometimes promised their support to both sides of the conflict. Considering the cavalier treatment they had suffered at the hands of the "superior races of Europe," one can empathize with the Arabs who eschewed fair play in favor of advantage and pay-back.

At the war's end, the once-again victorious Allies, perhaps aping the mendacity and double-crossing they had encountered from many Arab leaders, reneged on many of their own promises. This was the time of the Balfour Declaration, then the first attempt to establish the state of Israel, and the subsequent formation of terrorist groups in Palestine—this time, however, they were Jewish, and the enemy was Great Britain.

Great Britain, staggering from the awesome ravages of six years of global warfare, besieged and bedeviled by the seemingly systematic collapse of its empire, was unable to contain the flickering fire of Zionism in Palestine and in 1948, by virtue of United Nation's Resolution number 181, the state of Israel was born. The possessors, the Palestinians, became the dispossessed and were driven or fled from Palestine into surrounding Arab states. Isolated from the general conduct of life by their settlement into Palestinian refugee camps, those Palestinians became the genesis for what today we call Middle-East terrorism.

My own close, personal observation of both Jews and Palestinians has led me to the conclusion that they share some remarkably similar traits. The persecution of Jews for two thousand years has to have its motives in secular rather than religious fears.

By whatever genetic strain exists, maybe the theory of survival of the fittest or by whatever means, Jews shine intellectually in science, the arts, and commerce. Their one area of weakness, in my view, is an attractive one; they seldom fare well in international politics. I suspect a deep sense of justice and fair play precluded success in that arena. Whatever the reason and whatever the circumstance of society and wherever the location, Jews have always led the local population in success in the aforementioned fields of endeavor.

TERROR IN THE SKIES

The indigenous Germans, Poles, English, Russians, or whomever they found themselves among, envied and feared their success and intellect. The Jews became targets over and over again, targets for bigotry, envy, greed, and fear.

Within the Arab world the Palestinians hold a similar position. Scattered throughout a number of lands and nations, confined to ghettos known as refugee camps for three generations, refused and denied assimilation into the indigenous society they live within but are unable to share, they are feared for the same reason Jews are feared. They dominate the sciences, arts, and commerce and, furthermore, in one-upmanship on their Jewish cousins, have displayed some ability in the field of politics.

In their relatively short history of being the dispossessed, they have suffered persecution, bigotry, envy, greed, and fear. On at least two occasions they have been driven from their host nations, Jordan and Lebanon, at gunpoint and have at times suffered the mass slaughter of their people because of their nationality.

All of this provided the perfect breeding ground for terrorism, terrorism against those whom they hold responsible for their fate and also against those who support them. There is an old Arabic saying traced back to the eighth century that states: "Any enemy of my enemy is my friend and any friend of my enemy is my enemy."

This is a philosophy the Palestinians have practiced to excess. From the breeding grounds of the refugee camps came the Palestine Liberation Organization (PLO) under the leadership of a curiously non-charismatic individual called Yassir Arafat. A physically unattractive man with only a moderate command of language and rhetoric, reportedly of unusual sexual preferences, he, nevertheless, caused Palestinians throughout the Arab world to unite under the banner of the PLO.

The history of the PLO has been as internally violent as its acts against its enemies. George Habash, head of the splinter group Palestinians for the Liberation of Palestine (PFLP), the Black September group, Leila Khaled of hijacking fame, have all played significant roles in the advancement of the PLO cause and then its diminishing role in the political scene of the Middle East.

To some, Arafat has become an Arab Flying Dutchman, condemned to travel forever without home or port in which to rest or seek shelter. Arafat's diminishing role and that of the PLO created a vacuum that many have rushed to fill. Regardless of country of origin (Arabic or non-Arabic), regardless of race, the common thread that binds the most currently significant breed of Middle-East terrorists is the thread of Islam.

Since the end of World War II, figures such as Mohammed Mosadegh of Persia, Nasser of Egypt, Quaddafi of Libya have dreamed of a Pan-Islamic world with Mecca as its center, just as the Vatican is the center for the Catholics of the world. Unlike the Catholic religion, however, these Islamic religious leaders wish to impose secular authority on all who live under the banner of Islam.

The fervor of Islam is so great that much of it is spent on terrorism or warfare against itself as disparate sub-groups of Muslims struggle for dominance. Shiite, Shia, Sunni; the list of brands of Islam is long and its page is bloodstained. There is, however, one element that in a sense draws them together, and that is the sometimes deep and passionate hatred for Judaism, Israel, and those who support either or both.

This is the catalyst, the match that lights the fuse of terrorist response.

MIDDLE-EAST TERRORISM began in the seventies, and the terrorists enjoyed a large measure of success, much of it a result of the unpreparedness of their targets. Airliners were unprotected against attack, embassies were still considered sacrosanct, British, French, or U.S. companies overseas were most welcome and much sought after; and they all were available like so many, large, fat, choice sitting ducks. These were the good old days when the air was clean, and sex was dirty; Coca-Cola, IBM, and ITT had yet to become dirty words. It was an age of international naïveté paradoxically mixed with some of the best international policies ever to emanate from the United States.

It was at this time that the Israeli/Palestinian conflict became a problem for much of the world.

At first there was a dash of romanticism about it. The smouldering dark beauty of Leila Khaled, automatic weapon in hand, evoked Hollywood-simulated images of dashing feats of derring-do of the romantic underdog against the larger, less romantic foe.

At least we know that Leila Khaled was real, something that cannot be ascribed to her fellow terrorist, the shadowy Carlos, not at least with any certainty. Reportedly from either Central or South America, Carlos could have been born from the pen of Robert Ludlam. Embellished by the Jackal, a product of the

Arab James Bonds or Psychopathic Killers?

mind of author Frederick Forsyth, the image of the secret will-o-the-wisp grew large in the public mind.

Among the legend and the myth was an element of truth. Indeed, a Carlos did exist and, indeed, he had conducted some terrorist acts and assassinations, but his ability to change appearance and freely travel the world, his dedication to a cause and his immortality were all the product of the media, prompted, some think by a public relations effort by the PLO worthy of a Hollywood flack. The terrorist achieved the pinnacle of success and recognition by becoming fashionable with the European jet set.

In November 1974 the world saw the spectacle of Yassir Arafat, gun on hip, addressing the General Assembly of the United Nations. In a very real sense, at the time he spoke he had blood on his hands, blood from victims who came from many of the nations whose U.N. representatives listened to and applauded him.

Arafat, Khaled, Nidal, Carlos, Habash are all familiar names. They are the leaders, the planners, the organizers; but are they the terrorists you are likely to meet if you ever fall prey to such a situation? Almost certainly not, for they now remain well concealed and safe from harm in the sanctuaries provided by their allies in the Middle East. They do the planning and avoid the execution of their plans.

The terrorist you will be most likely to meet if the staggering odds turn against you will be a pimply faced youth between sixteen and twenty-two years old. Pumped up by propaganda (and sometimes by drugs), he or she is probably as frightened as you are. He, too, is engaged in an enterprise that could cost him his life in a very violent way, and his reaction to the possibility of death is just the same as that of any other young person. *He has no great desire to die and most likely desperately wants to live.*

To be sure, these young terrorists are highly dangerous, but they are dangerous in the same way a child armed with a cocked grenade or automatic weapon would be. Like children placed in positions of authority or superiority, they can be both terrified and cruelly advantaged by it. Such uncertainty is characterized by the mood swings they go through during a terrorist operation and their childlike compliance and acceptance of the inevitability of their fate if they are captured by the authorities (their elders).

The killing of Leon Klinghoffer on the *Achille Lauro* and the brutal beating death of Robert Stethem, the American sailor on TWA #847, both in 1985, are bloody testimony to the unsophisticated nature and training of these terrorists. These seemingly senseless and unnecessary killings are essentially ritualistic murders designed to build their morale, "blood" themselves, and terrify others. It's like a child who kills a bird with his first pellet gun. The quick arbitrary shot, the death, the fright, and the remorse.

They seldom survive or get to perform more than one mission or operation, and consequently the next batch is just as green. Those that do make it tend to be promoted to what might be termed "the officer ranks" and are used in training, planning, or leadership roles and situations. Terrorists who operate as frontline troops are seldom veterans.

Bear all of this in mind if you ever fall victim to them, for it will help you cope with the situation and help you survive. Remember their fright and uncertainty; remember their

Arab James Bonds or Psychopathic Killers?

vulnerability. This will put them in perspective and will give you hope when you think of the formidable sophisticated array of international response that is poised to rescue you.

WHILE YOU AWAIT that rescue here are some very practical suggestions for you to follow to ensure that you are there to enjoy the rescue:

- Pay attention and listen carefully to the instructions of the terrorists.
- Follow those instructions carefully and deliberately, and avoid any sudden moves.
- Don't argue or ask questions, and never, never volunteer to do anything.
- If you are accustomed to authority, conceal it and display nothing but compliance.
- Unless directly spoken to, avoid eye contact with the terrorists. This is especially important in the early part of your situation when tensions are high in both the terrorists and their victims.
- If they rob you, don't resist physically or verbally. Hand it all over, for you should never be carrying anything more valuable than your life.
- Do not ask for anything *unless absolutely necessary*. Trips to the toilet and access to medication are about the only things you should request permission for. And make sure you ask before you make such a move.
- Keep your thoughts to yourself, and avoid talking to your fellow hostages. (They may be sleepers, or your communications may be viewed with suspicion by your captors.)

- Accept any food or drink that is offered to you. Avoid drinking alcohol, even if it is offered to you, but instead put it aside as you want to be alert.
- Stay aware of what is going on around you. Do not retreat into a cocoon. Use the time to assess the situation and conjecture about possible scenarios and how you may react to them.
- Get yourself mentally prepared for questioning or interrogation by the terrorists. If you are someone who would be particularly useful to your captors, try to conceal it; otherwise be as truthful as you can be.
- Apply the old axiom of dinner party conversations; avoid any talk of politics or religion. Offer no support or opposition to the terrorist cause. If asked, act dumb and say you know little about the matter. If they wish to educate you, let them, and listen quietly.
- Avoid planning or making escape attempts unless you are *absolutely certain* that you will succeed without any adverse consequences for you and your fellow hostages.
- Use the time to repeatedly prepare yourself for what you will do if the situation deteriorates to the point where violence is begun by the terrorists and/or armed intervention takes place.
- *If this situation arises, get down on the floor as quickly as you can and roll your body into the smallest ball you can make and stay that way until you are told it is OK to get up and move.* (Special hostage rescue forces are trained to shoot at targets that move and are upright.)

If you are rescued from any hostage situation, allow yourself

Arab James Bonds or Psychopathic Killers?

to be treated by a trained psychologist or psychiatrist. Trauma may be so well hidden that it is concealed from yourself.

Having said all that, it is important to remember that your chances of having such an experience and needing this information are very, very remote. Living is hazardous to your health; indeed, we read of the poisoning of our environment, the drug epidemic, violence on the streets and in the subways, rejection of traditional values and in general, the world going to hell in a hand-basket.

What we must also focus upon is that people are living longer, new cures for diseases are being found, the aging process makes humans of teenagers, charity and kindess still abound both on personal and institutional levels, and, if you believe in God, that He most certainly loves you.

Ever since man first ventured beyond the range of what could be seen from his cave, travel has fascinated and delighted the human species. Stop and think of the extraordinary ability we have to see and smell and live and understand and delight in traveling to foreign lands and places.

International terrorism has unfortunately become an accepted fact of our time so you can't ignore it, nor should you try to do so. Instead, understand it and put it in perspective, and do not allow it to change your way of life or your plans for if you do, then the terrorists have won and you and civilization have lost, and life will be the worse for it.

10

Command Under Fire: The Pilot's Role

Probably the primary reason I became involved in the subject of hijacking and terrorism was because I am an airline pilot. As in many other professions that evoke a certain sense of hazard or excitement, pilots tend to have an affinity for each other, an affinity that transcends national identities. Tales of displays of camaraderie between enemy fighter pilots abounded during World War I.

Airline pilots, by the international nature of much of their work, feel most comfortable when around and among other airline pilots, regardless of nationality. Police officers have the same propensity to have instant rapport with others of their profession, regardless of where they are from. This feeling probably stems from sharing the same environment, one with dangerous elements that catch the unwary and the unprofessional.

When an aircraft got hijacked in dramatic circumstances, I confess that my first thoughts used to be for the captain of the hostage flight. I wondered what he must be feeling to have his almost absolute professional command authority torn from him by some maniac with a gun or bomb. What sense of anger and frustration there must be to have his beautiful aircraft placed in jeopardy by some low-life with a bottle of gasoline and a cheap lighter.

As I became more and more embroiled in the maelstrom of hijacking and its ultimate metamorphosis into international terrorism, much of the anger and frustration in me became directed against those in the governments, airlines, and international areas who refused to do anything about it.

The weakness and cowardice of many countries in the United Nations in the late sixties and early seventies caused the world to plunge headlong down the path to a place where international terrorism replaced justice, negotiation, and compromise. Many so-called advanced nations such as France, Italy, Austria, just to name a few, fiercely resisted attempts by airline pilot organizations to institute a new, international protocol for terrorist attacks on civil aviation that would effectively repudiate and isolate from the civilized world those who supported or committed such crimes.

By 1971, the pilots of the world had seen the handwriting on the wall and were forecasting the escalation in number of attacks as well as their magnitude and body count. In the United States a small group of airline pilots within the Air Line Pilots Association cast about desperately to get someone to listen to them. As chairman of that group, I felt that public awareness was not enough; we had to get the attention of those in the international community who could do something about it: the United Nations General Assembly.

Desperately short of funds, we cast around for a way to get to those people. Out of a conversation over a couple of beers one night, an idea was born. It was ambitious and it would be costly, but we felt it could be done. Thus was born the idea of the T+ flight.

T+ was the slogan meant to signify the Tokyo Convention on Unlawful Seizure of Civil Aircraft plus the ancillary treaties of Hague and Montreal, which also dealt with the subject matter, at least in part.

We decided we would rent ourselves a Boeing 747 (then a fairly new phenomenon on the aviation scene), crew it with pilots and flight attendants who had been hijacked, and take the entire General Assembly of the United Nations and their spouses on a flight from New York to Montreal, home of the International Civil Aviation Organization. There we would host a luncheon, have the delegates and guests addressed by those crew members, who would relate the details of their terrifying ordeals, do a little preaching at them about the damnation that was ahead if the world didn't change its ways, and then fly them back to New York in time to get home for dinner.

Because of what we felt was a rapidly deteriorating situation in civil aviation, we determined that we had only three weeks to pull it off. Using ALPA's office in New York City, pilot volunteers began making calls trying to raise funds for the T+ flight while others attempted to get an airline to pull a Boeing

747 out of service for a Saturday and lease it to us for at least eight hours from 10:00 A.M. to 6:00 P.M.

Contracts for the feeding of over five hundred people at a lunch in the Montreal Airport Terminal restaurant had to be negotiated and signed, and special permission for international transit of a mass of diplomats had to be sought.

In retrospect, examining all the obstacles that were known and the number that were actually encountered, common sense would dictate that it couldn't be done. There was one ingredient present, however, that helped those of us involved to brush those problems aside: the bumblebee factor.

Every pilot in the world knows that an aerodynamic analysis of a bumblebee with regard to its weight, size, shape, and body surface in relation to its wing span, wing area, and motive power will scientifically reveal beyond any argument that the bumblebee cannot fly. The bumblebee, of course being unaware of this scientific, aerodynamic, mathematical fact, goes ahead and flies anyway because he doesn't know any better!

We are counting very heavily on the good old bumblebee factor, and it seems with good reason; for some twenty-odd days from concept, thirty-five thousand dollars and a leased Pan Am Boeing 747 later, on November 6, 1971, the T+ flight containing more than 90 percent of the United Nations General Assembly took off from John F. Kennedy Airport in New York bound for Montreal.

Those twenty days of organization, preparation, and sometimes desperation passed in such a frantic blur that no real record of events was made. Memory alone provides any details of that period, and much of that has dimmed over the years; but I do remember one particular incident when I called a senior management official of American Airlines seeking a contribu-

Command Under Fire: The Pilot's Role

tion to the cause. He replied, not unkindly, that hijacking had not been a problem for American Airlines and while he wished us well nothing more than his good wishes would be forthcoming.

The very next day, American Airlines had what was to be only the second Boeing 747 hijacked at that time and taken to Havana. The same official called me at the ALPA New York office and said "I don't know how you arranged it, but we have got the message. We pledge $5,000.00 to the cause."

IN AND OF itself, the flight was a huge success. George Bush, then U.S. ambassador to the United Nations, helped us host the several hundred dignitaries, and flight attendants from half a dozen airlines mingled among the extraordinary manifest of passengers serving drinks, snacks, and stories of their hijacking experiences. There was almost a carnival air about it. Not being qualified as a pilot on the Boeing 747 at that time, I was unable to be part of the cockpit crew, so in concert with many of my hijacked pilot colleagues, I hosted events in the cabin.

Throughout the whole flight I was deeply worried about two things. My primary concern was, not surprisingly, security. Here I was with probably the most newsworthy, important international group ever assembled outside of the General Assembly Chamber of the United Nations, and I had them confined on the prime target of choice for any terrorist or hijacker. Remember, this was 1971, and magnetometers and X-ray baggage checks had yet to be developed. We were unable to check our VIP passengers physically, all of whom had diplomatic immunity. I can only assume that the bad guys were as unsophisticated and unprepared as we were, for I can see, today, Abu Nidal or Arafat or a multitude of others who would drool at such an opportunity. There were no security incidents; however, one or two diplomats and some accompanying family member or staff overindulged in the free booze, disarmed perhaps by the novelty of the whole thing. Only when the last one deplaned that evening, back at Kennedy Airport, did I relax, get out of uniform, and have a stiff drink.

My second concern was for some of my own organizers. A well-meaning but unthinking pilot volunteer had allowed that it would dramatically underscore our plight if we were to pull a mock hijacking!

I was well aware that a majority of the diplomats would be armed or have bodyguards accompanying them. The idea of someone jumping up, waving a weapon and declaring "This is a hijacking" was so preposterous that it appealed to many of the volunteers who were frustrated and angry by the lack of response from the international community.

I pointed out that the resultant shoot-out between diplomats, bodyguards, family members, security, and law-enforcement personnel would make the gunfight at the O.K. Corral look like a minor disagreement among friends. There would be chaos as good guys shot it out with good guys, not knowing who was who.

I had so much difficulty in squashing that particular idea that during the entire day I walked around with the terrifying thought that one of my people would do it anyway; airline pilots by their very nature are very strong willed and self-assured and don't take orders too easily.

Fortunately, they also recognize good sense when they see it; so the day passed without any dramatics other than those that came from the stories the diplomats heard during the time on the ground in Montreal. Pilots and flight attendants spoke to that assembled crowd of dignitaries and quietly and forcefully related their experiences. I can recall one National Airlines captain who had the dubious distinction of having been hijacked three times! The delegates listened intently and seemed genuinely moved by what they saw and heard.

On the flight back to New York I heard many expressions of support for the idea of a new protocol that would deny these hijackers, these criminals and pirates, sanctuary. Alas, history has shown that while those men and women were well intentioned, it was evident that the governments that they represented mostly did not share those intentions, and we found ourselves back at square one again.

We learned much from the T+, however, as I stated earlier. The seemingly impossible can be done and done well, but I guess the most important lesson we learned was not to place any further reliance upon the United Nations to solve our international problem. We were able, therefore, to turn our energies and resources to more productive avenues of endeavor. We also learned that when things got to the stage of actually doing something, we were on our own and would have to take things into our own hands. It was from this that the attempted shutdown of the aviation world on June 19, 1974, came about.

Since that time I have held the United Nations and its so-called principles in disdain, having learned that, indeed, it does deserve the name it has made for itself: the Valley of the Winds.

DISAPPOINTED BUT UNBOWED by their dramatic but unsuccessful foray into the world of international diplomacy, the pilots of the Air Line Pilots Association began casting about for an alternative.

Many years earlier I had read some words by the great British writer H. G. Wells, who had in many ways prophesied the future. In 1936 he had written: "The problems of the world would not be solved by diplomats or statesmen, they would instead be solved by aviators for aviators recognize no boundaries, artificial or natural, for they cross them all with equal ease; and they speak a common language."

It was in these words that I found the inspiration to go on. We recognized that we could not stop hijackings by force of law; so we had to stop them by physical means of defense. This was the genesis for what would become known as pre-board screening. It could also be viewed as returning the authority to the captain, a perception that helped us gain a lot of support from pilots throughout the world.

It has become fashionable to view airline pilots as overpaid and underworked prima donnas, an attitude encouraged by airline managements. Yet when one reads the history of the war against hijacking, as in all threats to civil aviation, the airline pilot was on the front line, in the research lab, in the pulpit, and always ahead of anyone else. The airline pilots' self-imposed responsibility to be the last line of defense for the airline passengers has all the force and weight of religious convictions.

When the United States carried out the April 1986 raid against Libya, airline pilots in the United States and many throughout the world felt like standing up and cheering. I was actually in London attending the Annual Conference of the International Federation of Air Line Pilots Association when the raid occurred. Pilot delegates from nearly fifty nations were in attendance. The day prior to the raid I had briefed the conference in closed session on the current and forecast security situation in what turned out to be a grim and emotional session. Other than what I believe to be knee-jerk anti-Americanism, the general response was positive, and a feeling of "At last someone has had the courage to do something" prevailed.

As the news of the attack came in the morning, London time, it was the only topic of conversation at the breakfast tables in the hotel coffee shop. A delegate from France stopped by my table and, borrowing from a phrase I had used the day before in my closed-session briefing, inquired how I felt about innocent Libyan women and children being killed and maimed. I recall looking at him coldly and responding, "As you will doubtless find out, as you sow so shall you reap."

When a wave of terrorist bombings paralyzed Paris six months later, I wondered if he remembered what turned out to be my prophetic words.

HAVING BEEN VICTIMS more often than people in any other occupation, airline pilots take a singular view of terrorists. An eye for an eye is probably the most quoted sentiment, and there is strong support for any military or punitive action against those who would violently disrupt the peaceful commerce of civil aviation.

It has become deeply personal for them and has added to the already heavy burden of training, responsibility, and decisions a captain of a modern jet airliner has to cope with today. Not only does a captain have to concern himself with the condition of the aircraft, the amount of fuel, the weather at takeoff, en route, destination and alternate airports, he or she is now obliged to check security of the flight and aircraft, train in recognition and handling of explosive devices in flight, train in hijack management and criminal psychology, and frequently put all this training and knowledge into play while speeding through the air at 700 mph at 40,000 feet.

Put yourself in his or her place, and you can perhaps understand the anger, the frustration and, yes, even the fear.

In the final analysis though, we are sure of one thing: we will never relinquish command of the skies to terrorists, and we will not rest until our industry is safe from attack. Until that time comes we will use all the defensive weapons at our command. We may decide to cease flights into airports we consider to be unsecure or unsafe and, indeed, we have had pilots make such refusals in the past. Their airline managements have tried to discipline them for such actions but have always retreated at the threat of the adverse publicity that ALPA ensured would follow.

The terrorist war is bound to continue for some time, the attacks coming in bursts following the inevitable relaxation of security that occurs during a hiatus of such attacks. Keeping the watchdogs vigilant is a difficult task when their quarry is absent. Like freedom, the price of security is eternal vigilance.

Overstimulation of the security network can have similar debilitating effects. The "cry wolf" syndrome occurs especially in the area of bomb threats. Any fool with the price of a telephone call can make a bomb threat. We have had cases where passengers en route to an airport, late for their flight, have called in a bomb threat so as to delay its departure. I know

Command Under Fire: The Pilot's Role

of one case where a flight attendant in similar circumstances did the same. That flight attendant was traced and severely punished.

What can airlines do about this extremely vulnerable area?

THERE IS A profile for bomb threats just as there is for hijackers. Its purpose is to establish the validity of the claim—real or spurious? If the tendency points toward real, security experts must then ascertain if it is likely. I will not reveal how these processes work but will say that a gratifying degree of accuracy is attained in these assessment processes.

If the threat is considered to be specific and real, then, if the aircraft is in flight, the captain is informed by radio. The final decision of what to do next is in the captain's hands, although the entire array of airline and government expertise is at his or her disposal.

Frequently the call comes when the aircraft is over an ocean, which leaves very few alternatives other than to turn back or proceed to one's destination or the nearest suitable landing field. I can recall an incident many years ago when flying for Qantas. I was the copilot of a plane heading from Sydney, Australia, to Honolulu; we had just reached the point of no return or P.N.R. as we called it in those days. That rather dramatic sounding but entirely prosaic term indicates that point on your flight plan over water or desert where it is just as prudent in terms of flight time to continue to one's destination as it is to turn back to one's departure airport.

At P.N.R. we were alerted by company officials in Sydney via high frequency radio that a specific bomb threat against our flight had been received.

My captain was faced with a number of decisions. Should he continue to Honolulu or attempt to put down sooner at an unsuitable military airstrip on a Pacific atoll that was but a speck in the ocean. He had to weigh the risks of passenger injury and death that could result from a landing at such a marginal facility against the possibility that, indeed, there was a bomb and also that it had a timing device set to go off prior to our estimated time of arrival in Honolulu.

He decided to go on to the destination, and once having made that decision he was then faced with another. Do we say nothing to the passengers and keep them peaceful in blissful ignorance, or do we tell them so we can conduct a thorough check of every accessible part of the aircraft? A planeload of hysterical, panicked passengers is an ugly sight and can be extremely dangerous.

He decided to tell them and did so, after briefing the cabin crew in small groups in the cockpit. His briefing to the passengers over the public address system was masterful in its tone, calmness, and authority.

Leaving me and the remainder of the cockpit crew to perform the now mundane task of flying and navigating the aircraft, he lent his official weight and authority, in his full uniform including hat, to organizing the cabin crew and passengers in an inch-by-inch search of the cabin.

Identification of each and every carry-on item was made, lavatories, cupboards, overhead racks, seat pockets, every conceivable hiding place was methodically and carefully searched for the presence of a strange or out-of-place object.

The process consumed the several hours we had left to destination. For us in the cockpit it seemed like an eternity of

Command Under Fire: The Pilot's Role

waiting for the bang, the other shoe to drop, while in the cabin time flew by on wings (so to speak) as crew and passengers engaged in their busy tasks.

Having arrived within range of Honolulu and still no sign of the bomb, the captain returned to the cockpit and had to make another decision. After the landing roll, did he want to taxi the aircraft to an area where a mobile stairs could be used to assist in a normal, orderly deplanement of the passengers or should he order an emergency evacuation via the inflatable slides and risk almost certain injury to some of the passengers, particularly the elderly?

He opted for the mobile stairs. A thorough search by an understandably nervous ground crew revealed that there was no bomb on board the aircraft.

Some sick person had caused untold agony to a number of innocent people, created temporary havoc within an airline and at a major airport, and unnecessarily forced a captain to make decisions that could have endangered the lives of the crew and passengers.

MOST OF MY experiences relating to bomb threats since that time have revealed that over ninety-nine percent of them are false. Every so often, however, you will find a real one, and that's the one that gets your antenna quivering for the phony ones that follow.

One of the most bizarre bombing cases I can remember was back in the mid-seventies. An extortionist was making threats to a major U.S. airline that he had placed bombs on certain aircraft and in exchange for a large sum of money would reveal the location of the bombs. As he had detailed and specialized information about the planes in question, details that non-airline or non-operational people would be unaware of or unfamiliar with, his threats were taken very seriously.

Exhaustive searches of the threatened aircraft were made. A bomb-sniffing dog of the New York City Police Department Bomb Squad also was used. That dog had previously leaped into instant fame in the New York tabloids for sniffing out a bomb in a crew bag of the type carried by pilots and stowed in the cockpit. The dog, a German shepherd named Brandy, subsequently found other bombs at non-aviation targets, thereby adding to her fame.

With the three suspected aircraft checked out and nothing found, they were put back into service. One of them was used on a flight from JFK to Las Vegas. A few minutes after the last remaining passengers and crew members had deplaned onto the ramp in the heat of the Nevada sun, a bomb blew the cockpit into scrap metal.

A thorough forensic study of the wreckage revealed a frightening fact. The bomb had been concealed in the standard first-aid kit that is strapped to the aft wall of the cockpit and *was sealed with the required lead seal.*

It was evident that we were dealing with an extortionist who had intimate knowledge and access to the cockpits of the airline's aircraft. This pointed directly to either a pilot or a mechanic. Though the FBI never found the perpetrator, word leaked out that they suspected a former pilot of the airline who had been dismissed for disciplinary reasons.

A calculation of the time the bomb exploded from the time the threat was received suggested that the clockwork device had failed on the first sweep but had made contact on the

Command Under Fire: The Pilot's Role

second sweep twelve hours later. First-aid kits and any other sealed compartments now have clear see-through panels on them to enable an examination of the contents to take place without breaking the seal.

THE PILOT'S WORLD of problems has advanced from those relatively simple days of crude devices to the diabolical age of destruction brought about by advances in technology.

As recently as the tragedy of TWA 840 on April 2, 1986, we are faced with micro-circuitry in combination with esoteric high explosives that can be set to explode at an exact time *weeks or even months later.*

When the sports facilities were being readied for the Summer Olympics due to take place in Los Angeles in 1984, there were serious fears that explosives could *actually be built into the structures,* with these timing devices set to go off at some significant time, such as the lighting of the Olympic flame, and have a horrified world of several billion people witness the resulting devastation live by satellite on their television screens.

Either it was not attempted or the excellent security that was embodied in the entire organization prevented it. For different reasons I would like both to be true.

I MENTIONED THAT TWA 840 was a victim of modern technology of destruction. There is little question that the woman May Mansur was responsible for placing the explosives under the seat prior to deplaning. Her public denials of such complicity followed the bombing, and doubtless you have observed that she has disappeared from sight. She and her terrorist cohorts know that she is marked for counterterrorist assassination as are her relatives. She and they will have to remain in hiding for the rest of their lives, which, given the quality of these counterterror specialists, may not be too long.

What happened on that flight, and how did the crew react?

TWA 840 was engaged in its daily round-robin flight that runs through Rome, Athens, and Cairo. This deadly triangle of terrorism is so well known that airline security there was reputed to be the best in the world—other than in Israel.

How then did Mansur smuggle the explosives on board? There is little doubt that she had the explosives with her when she boarded the flight in Cairo. She had gone through all the security checks that were in place at the time, but she still aroused some suspicion. The local security forces, finding nothing they could use to detain her and realizing that departure time was imminent, let her board without informing the captain of their suspicions. He could have made a decision to leave her behind or at least delay the flight to allow for a strip search. As the world knows, this did not happen.

The explosive used was most probably C4 plastic or Semtex, a plastic explosive made in Czechoslovakia and readily available to terrorists worldwide. The amount used was certainly no larger than a Mars candy bar and could have been shaped into any form and disguised accordingly to look like a powder compact, a passport, a small notebook, or, indeed, a candy bar. The detonator was probably the size and shape of a cigarette and undoubtedly disguised as one. It was charged by lithium wafer batteries, just like the ones in your calculator, and regulated by one of the devilishly clever timing devices I just wrote of.

Command Under Fire: The Pilot's Role

The whole bomb was probably broken down into innocent-seeming components to be assembled later in the lavatory and then slipped beneath the cushion of seat 10F.

Mansur left the flight at Athens, where, incredibly, she spent several hours waiting for a flight to return her to Beirut, which she had left early that morning to go to Cairo. She is therefore either a terrorist and did take the TWA flight with the express purpose of placing a bomb on it, *or* she is a singular masochist who enjoys airport terminals and flies just for the fun of it.

Several hours later, on what was an early descent into Athens—early in the sense that aircraft usually stay as high as possible for as long as possible to conserve fuel—the aircraft passed below the fifteen-thousand-feet level, and every pilot's nightmare came true—a bomb blew a hole in the plane, causing an explosive decompression and *unknown structural damage*. The cabin and the cockpit looked like the one described in the opening chapter of this book. Vapor, dust, and debris filled the air, along with the rushing noise and the screams of terrified passengers.

In the cockpit, the captain fought the controls, not knowing what had happened. The crew, emergency oxygen masks on, was running through the emergency descent checklist, calmly and methodically just as they have been trained a hundred times to do.

Back in the cabin, the flight attendants were in control of the passengers. They had every one seated and tightly strapped, but as they went about their duties they were grimly aware of that gaping hole in the side of the cabin through which at least four passengers had been sucked to a horrible death.

TERROR IN THE SKIES

As the aircraft got to a lower altitude, breathing became easier. The dust and debris were gone—sucked overboard. The cabin was still under control, although most of the passengers were in shock.

The captain used the word that he had hoped he would never have to use in his airline career—"Mayday"—as he contacted Athens's Air Traffic Control center for immediate emergency handling direct to the airport for a landing as quickly as possible. He had no way of knowing whether his plane had been so badly damaged that it could fail structurally. His touchdown at Athens was a particularly gentle one, so as not to put any further strain on the damaged fuselage. The ordeal was over, but the nightmare began, for this grotesque act was one that the surviving victims would carry with them forever.

This is especially true for the pilots, for in some indefinable way they will feel responsible. Over the years, on each and every flight, they have taken on the responsibility for the lives of the crew members and passengers who ride along with them.

If you ask them about it, they will pause for a while and probably respond: "I guess it goes with the territory."

In those few brief terrifying minutes on that afternoon of April 2, 1986, the pilots and the flight attendants demonstrated their worth in territory where no one should ever have to be.

11

The Worst of Circumstances

Elsewhere in the book I discussed the possibility of armed intervention by ground forces and mentioned the now-known existence of the elite groups in Europe and North America: the British SAS, the West German GSG9, the U.S. Delta Forces, and the Israeli Relief Commandos. The existence of these forces should be of great comfort to you for they are extraordinarily accomplished and effective. They are superbly trained in hostage rescue, and to say that they could snatch a bear cub from its mother's teat without her noticing it is probably true as well as being illustrative. Having seen them operate, I am full of admiration for their skills and would have great confidence *if I knew that they were available to rescue me.*

Unfortunately not all situations that deteriorate into the necessity for armed intervention occur within the geographic reach of one of these four groups, nor are they always allowed to operate on someone else's sovereign territory. In the case of Egypt Air Flight 648 on November 23, 1985, the question of sovereignty got in the way.

A force of troops from the Egyptian Army stormed the Boeing 737 as it sat on a distant ramp at the main airport of Malta. Twenty-two hours of negotiations had taken place, and the hijackers had shot five crew members and passengers, two of whom were killed.

In the rescue attempt sixty people were killed, including two of the hijackers, and thirty-five others were injured, some severely. This toll of dead and wounded is directly attributable to the fact that the Egyptian troops were not trained for a mission such as the one they were asked to undertake. They were certainly brave, but the orders to send them to do this particular task were foolhardy to say the least. Using traditional military or commando-type forces for hostage rescue, especially aboard aircraft, is like performing brain surgery with an ax, and, indeed, it will have similar results. Not only is the required training for hostage rescue aboard aircraft very special, but so are the armaments and equipment. Esoteric is the proper word to describe all facets of these special forces.

The carnage at Malta was terrible, and the tragedy of the rescue was only ameliorated by the heroism of the captain and copilot who were later awarded the Polaris Award for Heroism by the International Federation of Air Line Pilots Associations.

I HAPPENED TO be present to hear the first person report of one of the surviving passengers from the ill-fated Egyptian Air Flight #648:

The Worst of Circumstances

"At about 8 P.M. last November 23, I arrived at the Athens International Airport with a colleague, George Vendouris. We were on our way to Dubai, in the United Arab Emirates, to inspect one of the ships of the company for which I work. For some years I have been chief engineer for our company, and on this assignment George was to assist me.

"We were traveling to Dubai by way of Cairo on Egypt Air Flight 648. After passing through the various checkpoints, we reached the aircraft, a Boeing 737. Since we had only hand luggage, we were able to enter the plane relatively early. If I remember correctly, we were in row seven, seats A and B.

"Finally, after everyone had boarded, we took off according to schedule shortly after 9:00 P.M. The plane was not quite full, with fewer than a hundred passengers. Shortly after takeoff the flight attendants started serving soft drinks. We must have been twenty-five minutes or so into our flight when a man appeared in front of the pilots' door. He had a gun in one hand a green grenade in the other, and he started shouting in Arabic, but it became clear that this was a hijacking.

"So we followed the motions of the Egyptian passengers and proceeded to raise our hands over our heads. While giving orders, the hijacker was also trying to pull something out of the grenade with his teeth. He did not succeed, however, so he returned the grenade to his vest pocket.

"The hijacker, who, it turned out, was not alone, made those sitting in the front seats move back to sit wherever they could.

"Then he asked for our neckties. Next, the hijackers started to bring one person at a time to the front, taking his passport, frisking him, and then having him take one of the empty seats in front.

"When those in the front seats moved back, an Egyptian man ended up next to me. I learned later that he was in charge of the aircraft's security guards. When he was called forward, the hijacker took his passport, forced him to lie down, and then tied him up with neckties. Even before this, the plane's chief flight attendant had been tied up.

"When my turn came, following the Egyptian security guard, the hijacker just took my passport without frisking me and directed that I should sit down. He pointed to the right-hand side, about the third row.

IN-FLIGHT GUN BATTLE

"A few minutes later, there were gunshots just behind me. Immediately, we all ducked. Apparently the bullets depressurized the cabin, for the oxygen masks dropped from the ceiling. Many passengers put them on, but I didn't feel the need for oxygen. I believe that the captain had quickly brought the plane to a lower altitude.

"When the shooting ended, I looked back and saw the hijacker who seemed to be in charge lying down flat. He looked dead. Another man also was on the floor, and a couple of flight attendants and a passenger had been wounded.

"It seems that the hijacker had asked a man for his passport. The man turned out to be one of the security guards, and instead of reaching for his passport, he pulled out his gun and shot the hijacker. But the guard himself was shot by another hijacker in the back of the plane.

"The fallen security officer's gun landed at my feet and for a moment I thought of picking it up. But wisely I dismissed the idea—I would not have known how to use it anyway.

The Worst of Circumstances

"The pilot's door then opened and a tall masked man appeared with a grenade and a gun in hand. He spoke to the hijacker behind me, and then he looked straight into my eyes, motioning with his gun for me to stand. He said something, but from his gestures I only understood that he wanted me to drag the fallen hijacker to the pilot's compartment.

"When I started doing that, the hijacker motioned that I should turn the man over. Since I could not manage alone, the hijacker called someone else to help, and Demetris Voulgaris came. I had known Demetris for many years because he worked for our firm. Demetris took hold of the man's legs. I took the shoulders, and we turned him over. They wanted us to do this so that they could get the grenade from his vest pocket.

"After one of the hijackers took the grenade, we asked permission to give the fallen hijacker some water, but we were motioned not to. They probably figured he was beyond help. So we sat him up by the door, and we were told to drag the security guard forward. At this point, a hijacker saw the guns on the floor and picked them up.

"As we were bringing the security guard forward, we had in mind undressing him and providing him first aid. But when his head was close to the first row of seats, the hijacker told us to stop. I was ordered to empty two food trays—to throw the food on the floor. The hijacker said to put the trays on the first seat and motioned that I should hold the guard's head right there on the trays.

"It dawned on me that he intended to kill the wounded man, so I shouted, 'No!' And holding my hands over my face, I turned toward the passengers, saying, 'He wants to kill him!' Surprisingly, the hijacker did nothing to me. He held the security guard's head, but he did not shoot him. Then he sat down in the first row next to me.

"After a while I could no longer endure sitting there, so I held my hands up and moved toward the back, finding a seat somewhere in the fifth or sixth row. My young assistant, George Vendouris, came and sat behind me.

"The chief flight attendant, who had managed to untie himself, called out to one of the flight attendants who was being used to collect the passports. We were about to land. But before we did, the flight attendants were instructed to prop up and secure the hijacker, who was either dead or dying.

ARRIVAL IN MALTA

"Whether it was the hijackers' intended destination or not, we landed in Malta after a flight of about two hours. Shortly after the plane landed, the door was opened, and a doctor came on board. He was shown the lifeless hijacker and was told to examine him. The doctor did so, nodded his head, and motioned that he would move on to the body of the security guard. But the hijacker told him not to.

"All Greeks were told to sit on the right side of the plane where I already was. There were seventeen Greeks, of whom only five eventually survived.

"The attendant announced over the loudspeaker that all the Filipino women aboard should come to the front. Some other women also were invited to come forward, and altogether eleven women were permitted to leave the plane with the doctor.

EXECUTIONS BEGIN

"The flight attendant asked where the Israeli girls were. Thinking that they were going to be released, too, a young

The Worst of Circumstances

woman quickly responded. But when she reached the front, the masked hijacker grabbed her. He pushed her out the door onto the exit stairway, so I couldn't see what happened. But there was a shot, causing all of us to duck instinctively, and then a thud. The girl, we heard later, turned her head at the last moment, so that the bullet only grazed her. She fell down the stairs of the platform, hid under the plane, and eventually escaped.

"The hijackers, we later learned, threatened to continue shooting passengers unless fuel was provided. After a few minutes, the second Israeli girl was called, but she did not stand up. The flight attendant arrived with the girl's passport in hand, identified her, and told her to get up, but she wouldn't. So the hijacker sent two passengers whom he used as assistants because they spoke Arabic, and they forced her to the front. That was when all of us began to feel the shock.

"The girl was crying. She fell down and stayed on the floor. When the hijacker came out from talking with the pilot, he kicked her and pushed her outside. Again there was a shot, and a thud as she fell mortally wounded. By now it was a little past midnight.

"Shortly thereafter, three more persons were called, a young man and two women. From their names, we concluded correctly that they were Americans. The hijacker brought them to the front and had his two helpers tie their hands behind their backs with ties. They were told to sit in the front row.

"About an hour passed. Then the hijacker called the American boy. I must say that I was impressed by the boy's calmness. He stood up and walked up to the hijacker as if he were going to collect an award or something—very cool. Again there was the bang, the thud, and the door closed. Although I didn't see it, the boy also fell down the exit stairway. And, amazingly, as with the first Israeli girl, he, too, was only grazed by the bullet and survived.

"Another hour or so passed, and the hijacker called one of the American girls. She stood up, and the same story was repeated—the bang and the thud as she fell. By now it must have been about three or four in the morning. Rain was pouring, adding to the dreadful atmosphere of the night. The passengers were glued to their seats with fear.

"It was quiet—no crying, shouting, or other noise. But I could hear the muffled comments: 'Look, he's killed the Israeli girl,' 'That poor girl,' or, 'Now he's killed the American.' Also, the whispered questions: 'What is this?' 'How can this go on?' 'What will he do now?'

"As for me, during each execution I prayed to Jehovah. I asked that, if it was his will, he would remember the individual in the resurrection, so that the person could have the opportunity for life in God's new system.

"Meanwhile, the sun began to rise. The door opened, and the two who were assisting the hijackers went outside and brought in sandwiches. Some ate, others did not. They also gave us water.

"As the executions were occurring, we thought that the demands of the hijackers must be very high for those outside not to accept them. And we were thinking that any one of us could be the next to be executed. But as the hours passed after the American girl was killed, we began to believe that things were being negotiated.

"At about noon, the plane door was opened, and the other American girl was called up and shot dead. When this happened, again each one feared that he might be the next one selected for execution. But as the afternoon passed and night came, and nobody else was called up, we wondered if perhaps they had worked things out.

"YOU ARE TOO CALM!"

"During the day I thought to myself, 'This is Sunday and the public talk is now in progress in our congregation in Piraeus.' I said a silent prayer as if I were at the meeting.

"When the study would have been over in Piraeus, where I serve as a Christian elder, I said another prayer, placing myself in Jehovah's hands and telling him I was ready to accept whatever he permitted to take place.

"I thought of writing a brief note to my wife: 'Katie and children, we'll meet in the Kingdom.' But as soon as I took out my pen, I thought, 'What are you doing here? Playing judge? Didn't you say before that the matter is in Jehovah's hands?' I figured that I had no right to leave a note saying that I would die. So I put my pen back in its place without writing anything.

RESCUE AND ESCAPE

"Suddenly, at about 8:30 P.M., machine-gun fire erupted, evidently from outside. But gunfire came from the back of the plane, too, probably from the hijackers. We fell to the floor. An explosion followed, and all lights went out.

"'Since the lights are out,' I thought to myself, 'I can move now.' I stood up, but as soon as I did, I felt a burning sensation. It was some kind of gas, so I held my breath. I heard George say, 'Hey, they're going to burn us.' I couldn't talk myself, and I breathed as little as possible so as to survive.

"In the direction I was looking, everything was dark. But then I heard a voice, 'The other side.' I turned and saw a ray of light and headed in that direction. In a few moments, I found myself at an opening. It may have been an emergency exit over the wing. Whether I jumped from the wing or slipped, I cannot remember.

"The next thing I do remember was my lying down and someone standing over me, holding my head. I realized I was outside the aircraft and that these were probably our liberators.

"I started to breathe again. But even though there was fresh air, I felt as if I were still breathing gas. And it was that way for days afterward. Others had fallen behind me, and we tried to get up, but we were not allowed to. So we crawled behind some boxes. While there, we were searched. Then we were put in a car and taken to the hospital.

"Later we learned that most of the nearly sixty persons who died in the rescue attempt apparently died from the smoke caused by the explosives of the Egyptian commandos who had stormed the plane. Sadly, my colleague George Vendouris was among those that were killed.

AT THE HOSPITAL

"When we arrived at the hospital—it was St. Luke's Hospital—I heard the word 'Emergency!' We were put on stretchers, and a doctor came to see what was happening. I was stripped to my shorts. Then I was taken to one of the wards. I was in pain, and my eyes were bothering me. Soon I could see nothing at all, so I began shouting and a doctor came. He put something in my eyes.

The Worst of Circumstances

"They bandaged me and began intravenous feeding. I was washed with a towel and given injections for the pain. In my limited English, I told them that I did not want a blood transfusion because I was one of Jehovah's Witnesses. Then someone informed me that a Witness worked on the ambulance that had come to the airport, a Maltese Witness. When he came to talk to me later, he said, 'Don't worry, they won't use blood.'

"Finally, a doctor came. She was very polite. I could not see her, but I remember her voice. I asked if she would make a collect call to my home and inform my family that I was alive. I was worried about them.

"Someone came in who, if I remember correctly, said he was the hospital director. He took my hand and asked, 'What is your name?' and I told him. Later I learned that Witnesses from the Watch Tower Society's branch office in Greece had telephoned and were waiting on the line. The hospital director had come to see me to make sure I was alive so that he could tell them. This happened around daybreak on Monday.

"On Tuesday my wife and son came to Malta. When I felt her hand in mine, I knew it was my wife. I embraced her and offered thanks to Jehovah. My son came, too, as well as the manager of the firm I work for.

"During all this time I was being given oxygen so that I could breathe. Also, a nurse would come in, turn me face down, and hit me so that I would release phlegm. When I was able to see again, I saw that the phlegm was black. It must have been caused by the gases. On Wednesday my bandages were removed, but I could not take the light.

"When several reporters came that day, the doctor ordered them out. In the meantime, the police arrived and told me that I had to make a statement. Later they told me, 'You know so many details, you could write a book.' After that, a representative of the consul and a prosecutor came with a tape recorder and took my statement, again with the use of a translator.

"When this was over, my wife and son left the hospital. They stayed with some Maltese Witnesses until I was well enough to travel and we would leave Malta together. I am deeply grateful to be among the few survivors of the terrifying hijacking of Egypt Air Flight 648."

—As told by Elias Rousseas.

INDEED A CHILLING tale, made even more so perhaps by the simplicity of its telling.

I prayed that the world has learned a lesson about the use of standard military forces in situations such as this. I do know that if ever I fall prey to terrorists on my aircraft, I will do everything in my power to get the aircraft on the ground in a place where the real professionals can be used.

12

Welcome to the End of the Line

Throughout the book I have attempted to interest you, educate you, stir you, and reassure you.

As I pointed out, flying is a whole lot safer than almost any other mode of mass transportation. It has an air of glamour and excitement to it; and to most of us, the science of physics, which makes it possible for a craft weighing hundreds of tons to fly through the air with grace and speed, is nothing short of magic. Because of this magic, flying and its failures and disasters get more attention than they actually warrant. As was said, this is a prime motive for hijackings.

Since deregulation has happened to U.S. civil aviation and is spreading worldwide, some of the glamour is being lost in the drive to lower costs. This translates to less service, less convenience, and less luxury. Still in all, more and more people are flying for less money, apparently willingly accepting less comfort.

Travel, personal communication, and exposure to other lives and life-styles is the most effective means of creating understanding. Travel can do this, and aviation does it faster. It is a precious commodity to be preserved and nurtured. Attacks against it must be fought with the same vigor we fight diseases that attack our bodies; insects that attack our crops.

Like all pilots, I view terrorist attacks against civil aviation as a personal attack against me. I revel in the uniqueness of my trade, for no other gives greater freedom in exchange for grave responsibility, and I will fight to protect it.

One must take firm, swift, and decisive action against any attack on any means of long-distance transportation. Piracy on the high seas was virtually eradicated over a century ago. If piracy against civil aviation continues to be tolerated by established nations, then the rot will spread to other areas, and soon those who tolerate it will become victims. I am certain, however, that tolerance of air piracy will soon be passé.

Meanwhile, what are you, the air traveler to do? Having read this book, at least you have armed yourself with some simple but sensible protection. Next you should understand that *your* chances of death, injury, kidnapping, or mayhem as the result of a terrorist attack against civil aviation are minuscule. As I said earlier, living is hazardous to your health, so go ahead and travel, travel by air. Sit back and relax and have a wonderful time—thanks for flying with me, please come back the next time your plans call for a flight to somewhere and do be careful on the most dangerous part of your trip—the ride from the airport.